HAUNTED WATAUGA COUNTY,
NORTH CAROLINA

HAUNTED WATAUGA COUNTY, NORTH CAROLINA

TIM BULLARD

HAUNTED
America

Published by Haunted America
A Division of The History Press
Charleston, SC 29403
www.historypress.net

Cover images: Cone Manor in Blowing Rock, North Carolina. *Photo by Tim Bullard.*

First published 2011

Manufactured in the United States

ISBN 978.1.60949.215.1

Bullard, Tim.
Haunted Watauga County, North Carolina / Tim Bullard.
p. cm.
ISBN 978-1-60949-215-1
1. Ghosts--North Carolina--Watauga County. I. Title.
BF1472.U6B82 2011
133.109756'843--dc23
2011021477

CONTENTS

PREFACE

Lightning flashes, illuminating the backyard at midnight, and you think you see a body's shadow. The doorbell rings, so you answer it, and there is nobody there.

What frightens you? Spiders? Different people are spooked silly by different things. I put a rattlesnake in your sleeping bag an hour ago. Now we're going to see what scares you because I've been waiting my entire life to write a book that would keep readers up at night, disrupt their sleep patterns and make goose flesh rise just from reading a sentence.

Keeping my little nightmarish stories on the PG-rated side, I don't want to go overboard with obscene or graphic nature, but the result is hopefully going to make you jittery the next day—thinking things over, if you will. Reading ghost stories to two boys when I was a newspaper journalist, I would ask them what I am asking you now: "Do you want it not-so-scary or real scary?"

"*Real scary!*" the two boys would scream just before bedtime. Then, from a zero-gravity threshold, the story would take place from scratch, with no script, no back story and absolutely nary a prior thought—just off-the-cuff storytelling with a riveting ending. It was evident that my tale was getting a grip on their tender psyches because the covers would tend to creep up their necks, covering their noses as their eyes peeked at me. I never mentioned the swimming pool of blood. They were too young for "Turning Blind at Midnight" or "Lungs Full of Asbestos" and "Straddling An Electric Fence." Once I tried to slip in "Fish Hook Through My Eyeball," but I was scolded for going too far.

There are many haunted trails in the mountains around Boone. This fawn was captured by photographer Hugh Morton standing in a misty wooded area near Grandfather Mountain. It was in the Morton driveway, one day old. A twin died, but this one was accepted back by the mother. Hugh MacRae Morton (1921–2006). *Courtesy of Hugh Morton Collection of Photographs & Films, Wilson Library, North Carolina Collection Photographic Archives, University of North Carolina–Chapel Hill.*

But I always knew that my storytelling ability was growing stronger when they would beg after their longer-than-usual prayers, "Could you turn on the night light and leave the door opened a little?"

There are a lot of things that frighten me. As a journalist, I've seen bodies covered in blood. My articles have made people angry and caused them to threaten me. It's not paranoia—there has always been someone after me. Someone calls you on the phone and says nothing, only breathes. Would you spend the night in a graveyard?

The main thing that makes me bugged out of my mind is being on the first floor, looking at a window's curtains and seeing a silhouette outside, lurking. I have a recurring nightmare about that, and the door opens as a specter enters, laughing that loud, cavernous echo of a devilish chortle. Blood scared me early on, too. Snakes scare me. Quicksand frightens me.

The thought of being secretly poisoned sends me up the wall. I never saw a ghost—until my Aunt Bernice of Newton died. I saw her at the foot of my bed, and she was smiling. She didn't say anything, but I had felt her presence ever since the funeral, so I told my cousin, Jeff, about it, and he said that he had the same feeling.

Maybe we want to see people who have passed on so much that we conjure up spirits. I'm not sure. But whether it was a dream or not, one of my later stories cemented in my mind that there are ghosts and haunted houses. Facts cannot be ignored. As a journalist, I'm ultimately skeptical, and doubt fills my being as I cover first-day kindergarten stories, senior graduations, city council meetings and band recitals.

Drunk drivers scare me. The devil scares me. You have to believe in Satan to believe in God, especially in the world we live in. Boone and Watauga County have become the methamphetamine capitals of North Carolina, and if that doesn't scare you, nothing will.

According to VisitNC (www.visitnc.com; 1-800-VISITNC), there are three primary ranges in the state's mountain region: the Black, Blue Ridge and Great Smoky Mountains. There are 120 species of trees in North Carolina. The Appalachian Trail includes three hundred miles of winding passages. The highest mountain in the eastern United States is Mount Mitchell, at 6,684 feet, the bureau reports. One popular natural water slide is Sliding Rock in Transylvania County, with eleven thousand gallons per minute rushing down 67 feet of smooth stone into a 7-feet-deep pool. Doc Watson sings about the New River, which is the oldest river in the country and the second oldest in the world. Watauga County is God's country.

"The Blue Ridge Parkway, our nation's most scenic byway, stretches 250 miles in North Carolina from Cherokee and the entrance to the Great Smoky Mountains National Park to the Virginia-North Carolina border and beyond," reports the tourism agency. "The oldest stand of virgin timber in the eastern United States is in North Carolina's mountains at Joyce Kilmer National Forest."

North Carolina has more than one hundred wineries, ten lighthouses and 550 golf courses. "One of America's most baffling mysteries occurred near what is now Manteo," reports VisitNC. "In the 1580s a group of colonists sponsored by Sir Walter Raleigh suddenly and mysteriously disappeared without a trace. Their whereabouts remain a mystery today."

Wilbur and Orville Wright were the first to conduct successful powered flight on December 17, 1903, at Kill Devil Hills in Kitty Hawk. Pinehurst is one of the most famous golf meccas in the world, and the North Carolina

This photograph, taken by Hugh Morton in the early 1960s, shows the Blowing Rock, one of the most scenic overlooks in North Carolina, with its rock formations and majestic view. *Courtesy of Hugh Morton Collection of Photographs & Films, Wilson Library, North Carolina Collection Photographic Archives, University of North Carolina–Chapel Hill.*

Zoo is located near Asheboro, drawing thousands each year. A day trip from Boone is the Biltmore House (with its 250 rooms), a French chateau finished in 1895 as the summer home of George Vanderbilt.

When I was in school at Appalachian State, we'd stay up until dawn on Friday and Saturday nights in Eggers Dorm, listening to a radio DJ named "The Midnight Rambler" in Tennessee. Imagine yourself wearing a plaid mountain shirt and hiking boots, and you're there where we were. I'm going to tell you about Watauga County, an alpine Valhalla where cold is frigid and dangerous and the average temperature is sixty-nine glorious degrees. I heard it got so cold one day that a calf being delivered froze solid before it hit the ground. That's cold. Running out of gasoline is life-threatening.

"You're dead. You hear me? You're a dead man." That's what someone left on my answering machine once after I had done an exposé about criminals in South Carolina. I don't use answering machines anymore. It's not the threats you know about out there—it's the ones that you don't know about.

Ghosts are real. I did not believe in ghosts until I started this book, and in one of the tales there were irrefutable facts that told me that something supernatural was manifesting itself. I would not spend the night in a graveyard. Empty churches at night scare me. Can the dead send us messages from beyond life? I believe so. Why does death terrify us so much? The unknown sometimes proves to be something that is beyond our comprehension and explanation, yet it piques our interest until we feel there should be a complete investigation to prove the truth. When I was a patient suffering from diverticulitis in South Carolina, the pain and morphine became too much, so I asked nurses to tell me true, weird hospital stories. They said once a patient died on an upper floor; the only problem was that he was seen several times after midnight walking hallways.

Sometimes it is just time to call it quits for an endgame when you are a nonbeliever. Wiccans surround us at Walmart. It's what makes Hitchcock so beloved and Poe so unforgettable. When I was young, what kept me going back to the library was a stack of spooky stories. I would check out *Dracula* once a year and *Frankenstein*, too. Then I got into Poe. Spooky tales kept my thirst for reading alive. Reading the Bible was fun because there was a lot of material in there that was not only adult but was borderline psychotic, as well: killings, murders, nailing a guy up on a cross for three days until he succumbed. H.P. Lovecraft had nothing on that fable. I love being scared.

ACKNOWLEDGEMENTS

Rufus Edmisten.
Margo Metzger of www.visitnc.com.
The Frank C. Brown Collection of North Carolina Folklore, published by Duke University Press.
Watauga Democrat.
Boone Police Department.
Watauga County Sheriff L.D. Hagaman.
Charles Whitman.
www.visitnc.com.
University of North Carolina–Chapel Hill, Wilson Library.
Magellan GPS.
Julie Richardson.
Appalachian State University, Belk Library.
Dwight Sparks, *Clemmons Courier.*
Horn in the West.
Publisher Polly Lowman of the *North Myrtle Beach Times.*
Dr. Gray Bullard.
Mr. and Mrs. Bill Bullard.
Elizabeth Cook, *Salisbury Post.*
Sandra Shook, *Watauga Democrat.*
Villager Voice.
WRAL.
Winston-Salem Journal.

Diane and Conor Bullard.

The *(SC) Morning News* newspaper and Editor Jackie Torok.

WNCW and Pam Bunch.

Jessica Berzon, Ryan Finn and The History Press.

Mountain Witches

A man told the story that protection from a witch can come from hanging up a closed bottle. About thirty or forty years ago, the man said that in 1915 there lived in the Brushy Fork community an old man who was known to bewitch people, according to *The Frank C. Brown Collection of North Carolina Folklore*. His name was "Old Henry."

He was feared by everyone for miles around. Old Henry would supposedly cause those who perturbed him to have bad luck. Mrs. Polly Rayfield of Sharp's Creek nearby told the tale of this man. She allegedly had a good memory, especially from her younger days (taken from the Frank Brown folklore collection):

> *Once I went over to Brushy Fork to see Jim's wife. Jim's wife was durned powerful.* [Polly had heard that this woman was "bad off" so she went to see her.]
>
> *Her folks were there waiting on her, and none of them knew what ailed her. Only they said she had made Old Henry mad about something or another, and right then she was struck down sick. I didn't see nothing of Henry, but they were all powerful afraid he would come in there.*
>
> *Jim's ails got worse, when Old Henry came in the room. The family had put a doll up in the loft with a string close to her bed to scare witches out of the house.*
>
> *I didn't stay long because I was afraid Old Henry would be close, and I didn't want to set eyes on him.*

Witches can also be sent by a bad dream, people say, but it is unusual. A magic ring or circle made in the dust can be a tool.

Alex Tugman of Todd said in 1922 that under the spell of a witch crops may die or not mature. He said that pigs will not die but will allegedly stop growing or become smaller. Cows will not die but will not produce milk, either. Horses are often ridden by witches without being bewitched, some have it. In rare cases, a bewitched person is forced to crawl through briar patches and stones until he is exhausted. Cream for making butter can be affected by a witch. A coin can be put on the bottom of a churn to protect it.

My earliest recollection of a witch was Margaret Hamilton's portrayal of a real mean woman in *The Wizard of Oz* on the silver screen. Often a witch is portrayed as having a bony chin, long fingers, sharp fingernails and a black dress that she would wear while flying around on a broom. This word is particularly misused in a misanthropic way to describe some women, like teachers. In every community there are people who are weird just because they are single, live alone or do not share or talk with other human beings unless they run into them in public places. We play jokes on them and taunt them as kids and talk about them as if they are second-class citizens when, really, they only lack social skills. Have you ever visited the Salem Witch Museum in Salem, Massachusetts? It was in 1692, when witch hysteria gripped America; children were accused of dabbling in witchcraft and the dark arts. All it took was the daughter and niece of Reverend Samuel Parris of Salem Village to become ill in January 1692. William Griggs, the village doctor, was called, and later, nineteen men and women were hanged, with one man crushed to death and seven others dying in prison.

These were the days when even the sane people thought that the proper way a doctor treated an illness was to take a sharp object and slice a trench in your vein, letting you bleed a little.

THE HAUNTED SPRING

One mile east of the Watauga River, there is a spring on the roadside, according to Thomas Smith, where many ghosts are seen, and its reputation is known to many people, including a man near Zionville named Andrew Wilson, who provided the following in 1915.

The place's reputation was known to "scores of people." Wilson was a "reliable farmer."

I was coming from Elk Park one night about twenty years ago. I had been there with a load of timber. When I came to the spring where the ghosts are seen, I stopped to let my horses drink. The horses wouldn't drink, and they seemed like they were scared. Just then I looked ahead of me in the road and seen a man standing there. I could see he had shiny brass buttons on his sleeve like a soldier. Thinking it was somebody, I said, "Howdee." He didn't make no reply, so I spoke again, but it didn't notice me. I watched several minutes, and in a while I was gazing at the thing it just seemed to fade away, and I could never see where it went to. I tell you I drug off from there in a hurry.

But I didn't see the worst things that are seen out there. Lots of people have passed by out there and seen the strangest things you could ever tell of. They have seen seven possums cross the road that go into a laurel thicket near the spring then seven dogs right after the possums and then seven men cross the road right after the dogs into the laurel, and right after the men they have seen seven coffins sail across the road into the laurel thicket. Yes there was a man murdered there before the war. That's what causes those strange things to be seen.

Such narratives of the ghosts had been taken by those citizens who were well along in years but were told in good faith.

Dr. Rivers saw apparitions. His son was editor of the *Watauga Democrat* newspaper. Rivers was a well-known physician, and a few years after the Civil War, he was riding along the lonely road through the laurel just before daybreak. At a bend that avoided a fallen oak, he was surprised by a strange man on a gray horse, much like his own. Rivers was shocked to find no man or horse around the bend after they vanished just as rapidly as they had appeared. He rode to a farmhouse two miles away, where he told of his visitor. Locals believed this to be a sign of Rivers's death since he died shortly afterward. Why is the laurel haunted? Indians may have buried a tribal member there who was killed one summer.

There was a house between Cove Creek and Brushy Fork, according to records. Members of the community talked about a headless dog, but some say that long ago, when there were not many settlers, a traveler and his dog were murdered by robbers and that his body was buried under the schoolhouse. The dog in its spectral form would follow people who traveled past the schoolhouse. One man rode past the spot, and he saw in the light of a full moon a large black dog, which came down the bank. It followed him in the road, and the traveler sped up with his steed, but the canine follower kept up the pace and began to catch up, leaping up and riding the horse—and also having a bloody neck without a head. The dog finally vanished.

Three young men were also riding through once, and they thought that the story was a joke. Way down the trail, one of the men saw a large black dog following them, and he told his friends. They looked, and they decided that it was the headless dog because it cast no shadow on the ground from the moonlight. They went home as fast as possible, and the dog followed. One of the riders swung at it with a cane, and it went through the dog. They began to ride faster to a creek two miles away, and there it turned back.

Another tale from Thomas Smith is about the ghostly lights at night near a laurel:

Sometimes there's two lights, and then again there's three. They look just like candles, and they come sailing up the road towards my house 'til they get to that big gate below the barn. The night after anybody dies in the neighborhood, those lights just come and go all night. I've seen them, and dozens of others have seen them. The night after Herman Wilson's wife died, we seen those lights coming and a-going as long as we stayed awake. Sometimes they'd come to the gate, and then take down the branch and then again they'd sail out across that field yonder towards the laurel. I've always heard that Indians caused them things to be seen in the laurel. You know they used to camp all around about here.

Tweetsie Railroad has a "Haunted Tweetsie" event every October for the young cowpokes. The entire attraction turns into a Halloween extravaganza. It is located between Blowing Rock and Boone off U.S. 321. The cowboys on site ride around on horses.

Did you know some mountain folks think witches ride horses? One man in Wayne County said that witches rode his horse once a week at least, and the horse would be "wet with sweat," with a mane all tangled up. He nailed horseshoes over the door and the harness hook, and the horse was never ridden again.

Some thought putting a broom in front of a front door kept witches away. Some would get a new water dipper and drop a cup of water on the fire. Some turned the poker upside down to keep witches away.

The first run of the Halloween Festival Ghost Train at Tweetsie Railroad was in 1990. This attraction in Watauga County was named one of the top twenty events in the Southeast by the Southeast Tourism Society. *Photo by Tim Bullard.*

A Scene Near Boone is the name of this postcard published by the Asheville Post Card Company (1930–45); it shows the excursion route taken between Johnson City, Tennessee, and Boone, stopping in Doe River Gorge. *Courtesy of the N.C. Collection Photographic Archives, Wilson Library, University of North Carolina–Chapel Hill, Durwood Barbour Collection of North Carolina Postcards.*

Sometimes bewitched horses try to climb trees and walk fences and logs, and then they die. Sometimes horses do not have to be bewitched to be ridden by a witch. The way to tell a horse has been ridden by a witch is to look for its mane to be knotted and tangled.

"Witches have a natural antipathy for lye soap," Brown wrote. So you have to stir soap with a sassafras stick during the boil. Buttercream has a problem if witches are around, but put a coin in the bottom of the churn, and this "attracts the attention of the witch, and the butter will thus come."

There was an occurrence of a man who was supposed to be a witch, and folks wouldn't sell him anything since they were afraid of him and worried that he would cast a spell on them. One person reportedly asked the witch to sell him something, and the man would not do it, so the witch man went near the barn where the mother was milking, and about that time, the cow the woman was milking fell over. Two women, witch doctors, were called in, and they cured the animal.

The Baby's Ghost

A man told me this story, and I believed him. He is about fifty-four and six feet tall, with a beard, brown hair and blue eyes. He attended Appalachian State University (ASU) in Watauga County but dropped out. We weren't friends, but one night he shared his story with me over hot herbal tea in Boone. When I was first writing this story, I had a moment to think about how I could lay it out for the reader to sift through to leave one's feelings to the side and calculate the unreal from the real, the supernatural from our everyday, mundane lives. His problem is this. He hears a baby's cry. Not just every so often. All the time.

The last time he was on Howard's Knob, the largest mountain in Boone, North Carolina, he was with his wife. He told me the story. "Our wedding anniversary had just passed, and it was a very happy time for us because we had only been married a couple of years," he said, squirting honey from a soft plastic bear dispenser.

"With a sultry summer just passed, autumn was like I recalled from my days as a freshman at ASU in 1974," he told me. He said that it was an anniversary trip, dampened by rain that had caused them to pull down their tent off the Blue Ridge Parkway in Blowing Rock and head home. "I wanted to show her how majestic the view from Howard's Knob was over the football stadium, so we trekked up there, panting and sitting on a newspaper to keep our fannies dry," he recalled.

"Did you have kids then?" I asked.

"No," he replied. But they had not been alone: his wife was pregnant. "We talked about names. She would come up with the girl names. I came up with goofy guy names, and we picked out the furniture and paint for the baby room," he said as a Doc Watson song played over the restaurant's speakers. "We did all the stupid things, like imagining what it would be like to go fishing that first time or go to a ballerina recital the first time."

"That's not stupid," I chimed in, looking around the place in the hopes that I'd recognize an old friend. When you are listening to a story, you have to act interested, and that means eye contact. I usually look at the lips.

"We tossed about names. I think that was what my wife enjoyed the most. We bought up mostly a lot of diapers, which you can use on either flavor you wind up with. It's weird because all your life you spend trying not to run into pregnancy, but when you do, you tiptoe and start going to church like crazy. I had given up on church, but we became closer and closer after we ended up picking a religion."

"You make that sound like you were going to the grocery store to get some eggs," I said.

"Oh well, we discussed mine and her religion. She never had stopped going to church, but I would only go once or twice a year, definitely at Christmas with my family. It felt so good going back to church. Holding hands had a new meaning when she got pregnant."

He talked about how good health means a lot during a pregnancy, and that's when my mind drifted off, my cloudy, foggy eyes drooping as the tea kicked in. His face turned red. "When was the last time you went up Howard's Knob?" he asked me.

"With a buddy in college. We went up there during an eclipse once. It was so cool. We'd go up there when the windmill was working, too. It's a shame they took that down," I said. "You must have been really on cloud nine when the baby came."

Silence. The electricity flickered as waitresses blinked, looking at one another. Snow does that when it accumulates on the power lines. There's nothing like a Boone snow. It shuts college classes down if you're lucky, and then the trucks bring out the salt slush, and you play cards for days, homebound.

"Do you like Halloween?" he asked.

"Yeah! Of course! That's my favorite fun holiday," I said. "You get to scare the devil out of kids, put on a mask and be any monster you want to in the horror movie realm. You get to play a slasher."

"I hate Halloween," he said.

"Why? That's insane. The entire country of the United States of America makes a cottage industry out of October 31, pouring millions, billions of dollars into the economy just to celebrate everything evil. It's so antiestablishment."

Stirring his steaming tea with a metal spoon, clinking, his head dropped, and his hand went to his forehead as he sank. "Hey, man. What's wrong?" I asked.

"I used to love Halloween," he said, his head coming up, tears welling up. A person dressed as the devil walked in. So far there was a Frankenstein, three Draculas, one Nixon, three Wolfmen, a ballerina, a football player and some nerd dressed up like Harry Potter.

"What changed your mind?" I asked.

His eyes nearly rolled back in his head as he rubbed his face hard, so hard it became flushed red. "The day we were on Howard's Knob was one of the last days she was pregnant," he replied.

"Oh gosh, I think I'm sorry I asked," I replied.

"I'll make it short. This is the terrible part. I have nightmares about it, and that's not the worst part of it. It was Halloween, and she started feeling bad. Then came the blood."

"Oh my gosh," I said. "Get out of here. Durn."

He continued, "We got to the car, and I put down a few towels. We made it to the hospital, and we sort of realized what was going on. The next hour was the most awful hour I have ever experienced in my life. We held each other in the car and cried and cried and cried. It would not stop. Have you ever wept so long that it hurt? My eyes were stinging. We couldn't let go of each other. I wouldn't call it a hug. We were quite literally clinging on to each other for dear life, like the world was a lifeboat and an ocean storm was rocking us, about to spit us overboard like rats.

"Weary and our muscles aching from so much tension, we stumbled into the hospital, and before I knew it there were two women there, a doctor and a nursing assistant, and there was the brightest life in the world, shining in our faces. Her grip nearly pulled the tendons out of my wrist as the miscarriage took the tissue to another world."

His description really almost had me in tears because I had a family member who went through this, but I never knew it was so bad. I had always looked at a miscarriage as what it is: the most common type of pregnancy loss, with 10–25 percent of all clinically recognized pregnancies ending in miscarriage during the first thirteen weeks of pregnancy.

He and his wife had danced through the first part of this abruptly terminated event thinking that everything would be rosy, with no downside. Most folks don't know about dilation of the cervix and curettage to remove the contents of the uterus. It's called vacuum aspiration. Most women do not have to get a D&C, but our protagonist wasn't prepared for that, either.

"If you don't like heavy bleeding, you don't want to ever have one of these," he told me.

"I believe it, whew."

"It was hard on us. She was depressed for a long time, and I am bipolar, so my usual depression plunged me into an awful turn. Every doggone time you see a baby carriage, walk by a stack of infant clothing or hear a baby cry in church, you start crying."

"Oh my."

"It's really hard on the woman. She said not a day goes by when she doesn't think about it. And now that she has had her tubes tied, there's no going back for us. I think about it a lot, too," he said. "It's caused us a lot of emotional strife in our marriage. We've had so many arguments based on this. I've blamed her. She blamed her. We tried getting pregnant, but my heart just wasn't in it. We also tried adoption. When I think that I will never become a natural father, I sink so low, it's almost too hard to rise up. I'd sleep all day."

A baby shrieked in a highchair across the bustling restaurant. I got goose bumps.

"Every time I go back up to Howard's Knob, the wind will blow, whistling by my ears, creating a loud noise, and every time I will hear a baby's cry. Looking into the snowflakes, I can't see anything, but the sound is there. I feel our baby's presence. Sometimes I hear it in the house. I'll get up at 1:00 a.m. or so, and I'll run downstairs and look around. The noise will pass, and I'll go back to sleep."

"That's creepy, man. Maybe you need to talk to someone."

"Yes. I told my wife. She said I'm a mental case. There's some good news, though."

"What? Lay it on me. I need some after hearing that."

"Well we adopted."

"Whoa! You didn't tell me that. That's great, man! When? How old?"

"He's sixteen now, and he is the love of our life. He's precious. Whenever we complain about the miscarriage, he reminds us that we wouldn't have ended up with him, and we look at each other and smile."

"That's sweet."

"That's not the only good news."

A waitress dropped her entire tray for a six-top table, and the noise was gigantic.

"What is it?"

"Well you won't believe this. It's hard to describe how this happened. But you know how long I have felt that abortion was right and a good choice for women?"

"Of course. That's the truth."

"Well that night, it clicked on me, right in the car when we were locked in that embrace. I could almost feel our child ascending into heaven. Our baby was not just fetal tissue without a name. It had a soul, and it died fair and square, even though we never got a chance to see its face and hold it and comfort it when it was sick or feed it when it was hungry," he said. "I knew right then that no one could ever convince me that what we had created was not human life and that abortion must be wrong at any stage. I could never hate God. Terminating a fetus could never be right when we had lost our baby. I know that it was not 100 percent formed, but it was ours, and we were robbed, even though we tried not to blame God or each other, searching for reasons or sins for our punishment. We could only love life and search for more, and we did, and we found it—our son."

Outside, the snow had already piled up as a salt-sludge truck scraped the highway outside. The fresh snow was so white that it was hard to see imperfections in the cold night.

GRANNY FROME'S POWER

Why do young people and adults conjure up the idea that a woman can be a witch? Enchantment has been around since way before the Middle Ages. Shakespeare wrote about three strange witches in *Macbeth*. "I'm not a witch," a political candidate was known for stating in 2010.

"Bubble, bubble, toil and trouble," Shakespeare's witches chanted around a fire. The devil was a lost, lonely soul until witches came around. Two genders, two supernatural beings. The Salem witch trials show us that history can repeat itself as mass hysteria takes hold on the community's spirit. Rumors become fact, and people get strung up, dropping like sacks of flesh to droop, sag and drip until the last ounce of life is sapped out of the human body. Back in those days, it was hard to turn a community morsel of gossip back into the truth.

The Frank C. Brown Collection of North Carolina Folklore was compiled by Dr. Brown from 1912 to 1943, along with the North Carolina Folklore Society editor Newman Ivey White and others. It contained games, rhymes, tales, legends, folk ballads, beliefs and superstitions. When one is young, a tall tale can quickly turn into a rumor or superstition.

The collection was first published by Duke University Press in 1952. It contains some stories you would not believe, and most of them someone somewhere along the line repeated as truths. Brown (1899–1943) was a professor of English at Trinity College and Duke University. He founded the North Carolina Folklore Society.

I interviewed a woman recently, and later I learned that she was a bona fide witch. Wiccans are a dime a dozen these days across the landscape in

North Carolina and the South. Do you believe in sorcery? Is there really an occult? The idea that there can be a witch like in *Rosemary's Baby* has made a lot of money in Hollywood. There is an idea that there can be a good witch as well as a bad witch. What is the difference? So many millions of dollars have been earned from the *Harry Potter* series, which has catapulted witches and wizards into a cottage industry.

The devil has gone by different names: the Prince of Darkness, Satan, Lucifer and others. Margaret Hamilton may have nailed down the personification of America's favorite witch in *The Wizard of Oz* on the silver screen. Check out the Witch of Endor in your Bible. Go to I Samuel 28:1 and read it for yourself: rituals, paganism and worshiping the devil. When crops go bad, some farmers take it seriously. When someone spreads a disease, commonly it becomes known as a plague or an act of the Bad Man.

When you were small, what was your personal idea of the leader of hell? Mine was a guy with red skin, a beard, a mustache, a long tail with a leathery spear on the end, two horns in the forehead and long fingernails. He also had an Associated Press handbook on his desk and a football coach whistle around his neck. Just kidding. The devil could make you do whatever he wanted you to do—steal, cheat, lie. I saw his work once in Mullins, South Carolina, in a tucked-away farmhouse where the sheriff had summoned me on my day off (I had been imbibing). There were three people, murdered, in this crack house full of half-eaten, rotten food and old furniture. I had to burn my new Rockport shoes when I got home because the coroner said the victims had AIDS. He had been there. Fortunately, I don't remember much about it.

Superstition breeds fear of the devil and witches. Adults are guilty of it as well as young people. They ridicule the weird old guy or lady down the street, a single person with no friends and odd, filthy habits. There is usually a lot of junk in the yard, grass that grows wilder than in a jungle and maybe a rabid dog or two that barks at neighbors and pedestrians.

Just why witches were burned is an issue of either permanent disposal or merely fear, according to your ecclesiastical background. Some witches were drowned. There is indeed a Carolina Witch bait enhancer sold, a bright device used in fishing. Designed by Don Maples, the Witch Golf Club on the Grand Strand in South Carolina melds the icon with the links, a trance that has captured many a golfer.

Covens attract witches like frisky night flies to a bulb. If you hear someone say to you, "Blessed be," watch out—you've met a witch. Necromancy is what the Witch of Endor was accused of—raising the dead. Read up on the Code of Hammurabi, the Babylonian law code.

"Magic" is the first word in the dictionary used to describe witchcraft. These days, to fight witches one needs a lot of lawyers. Should Ouija boards be illegal? North Carolina had an anti-divination law, fifty-three years old, that was repealed in 2004. The granddaughter of Granny Frome reportedly recorded the following recollection, and the words were transcribed by a professor, W.A. Abrams of Boone, in August 1940. Driving a nail into a picture of a witch is called the best way to take care of her, according to the account.

"Yes, I reckon I can tell it to you," she said, taking snuff out of her mouth to talk. An uncle and Aunt Cindy lived in a gap about 1880. Witches had allegedly been bothering this couple for quite some time, she said, with one steer dying and other cows going dry.

"That was a sure sign of witches working," she said. Next one of Ed's best dogs just laid down and died, she reported, and that made Ed go "plumb off the handle" and say that he was damned and he would be damned if he would stand any more of it.

"Granny or no Granny, he would put an end to it," she said. "You see the witch was his own granny. She got mad at Ed about something or other, and that was her way of paying him back." Ed swore that Granny's picture was going on a young black gum tree before dark, promising that he would sink a nail in her picture.

Ed put a cross where the heart should be, she said, and he expected the witch to become ailing right away. If you drive the nail in, she would get worse and finally die unless she could borrow something from her.

"Ed was that mad. He swore the nail was going plumb up to the head," she said. Sure enough, the old lady got sick and asked for salt and tobacco and then kindling wood, with no luck. Old Granny Frome was about gone when Aunt Cindy started to feel sorry for her and asked Ed to take the nail out.

A rooster came and stood in the door and crowed thrice. Ed promised to keep doing what he was doing. At dark, Ed saw Granny coming over the ridge with her hand over her heart. Ed grabbed a handle and ran up the ridge to pull the nail out, but he was too late, she said. Granny got inside the gate and yelled, "You've killed me! You've killed me!"

At that time, Aunt Cindy took her a gourd of water, and the old woman grabbed it and threw it up in the air, exclaiming, "You've killed me, Ed Dodson, you've killed me! But I'm getting even with you now. My witch spirit, I'm leaving it here to plague you, Ed Dodson. As long as you live!" Her spirit went into Ed, and she was gone. He acted queer after that, she reported. "He was afraid of the dark," she said.

THE PHANTOM PILOT

Some days, when you hear the distant buzz of an airplane flying high above Howard's Knob mountain in Boone, the craft may fly into clouds and mysteriously disappear. That's Bob Kennedy saying hello. Bob was a great cop. He was a hero and a friend to all, but he is dead now.

What you are about to read is meant for your eyes only and is extremely confidential. Kennedy is dead, but his ghost lives on, his legacy as a police officer flying high and respected as a bona fide North Carolina hero from Watauga County. He had a sense of humor, and he had a family.

The Airborne Law Enforcement Association Fallen Hero Memorial lists Robert Kennedy thus: "End of Watch: Wednesday, July 17, 2002, Aircraft: Cessna 172."

Major Robert C. Kennedy was married at the time his plane crashed while he was searching for marijuana plants with Pilot Sergeant Anthony Scott Futrell of the Mecklenburg Police Department and Deputy Richard Edward Ashley Jr. of the Chowan County Sheriff's Department.

Kennedy was born on July 8, 1956, in Stanly County. He was the commander of the Boone Police SWAT Team and Dive Team and had a great personality, treating all who knew him with respect. Bob graduated from Pfeiffer University and the Federal Bureau of Investigation (FBI) National Academy. He was a member of the Civil Air Patrol. He also was a board member of the Underage Alcohol Initiative.

His friends may not have known his involvement in one case in Boone when he was a member of the Boone Police Department. This is when

Kennedy found himself face to face with a religious cult group that was recruiting members on the campus of Appalachian State University.

In the March–April 1981 issue of *The Way* magazine, there is a photograph of Dr. Victor Paul Wierwille at Washington National Airport. He has a tall chimney sweep–style stovepipe hat and a striped ascot. He and his wife are in Washington, D.C., to attend the inauguration of President Ronald Reagan, the magazine reported.

On one of those days in the early 1980s, I sat in the home of Detective Bob Kennedy outside Boone on a hilly section on the northeast portion of Watauga County. Bob kept a lot of firearms in his trunk. Last I heard, after having bumped into him at a narcotics convention in Wilmington, North Carolina, he was busting people in Boone, wearing very long hair as an undercover agent. A farmer with us named Nelms was an older gentleman, dressed casually; he held his face in his hands, with tears streaming down his cheeks as he choked back sobs. Bob and I exchanged glances, and I tried to get my mind off this unsettling scene afterward by watching Bob open up his trunk to show off some new guns to me.

"Take it easy," I told the farmer. "I know it's rough. I'm sorry about what has happened to you."

Under normal circumstances, a farmer from Castalia, North Carolina, would not cry in front of another man. He probably wouldn't weep in front of a woman, even his wife. But this man's mind was on his daughter, who had been a freshman at Appalachian State University until she met a member of The Way International after watching TV. "We have a solicitation policy on campus," responded a spokesman for the ASU Residence Life Department. "We treat everybody the same, whether they are a religious group or a political group or whatever. The problem is that many times the staff is the last person told that they're there." Complaints were made by students over Way members in the dorm.

At Gaston Lake, in the Piedmont area of North Carolina, deprogrammers counseled Nelms's daughter for a week, the farmer told us as Bob served us soda and pretzels. This disturbing experience was a bit distant from the halcyon days Nelms's daughter had spent in childhood at the Red Bud Baptist Church in Castalia. Nelms took a long drag off his cigarette, smeared its orange tip into the ashtray after the long day of court and told his side of the story.

"She told a different story up here today," said Nelms, then forty-five. I had been in court when Nelms sat among the curiosity seekers in the gallery. Nelms plowed many rows of tobacco in the humid fields of his farm in

Franklin County to send one of his two daughters to college; her name was Karen Rene Nelms.

"She had never given us any problems at all, always at church, dependable, good worker," he recalled, blowing smoke out his nose and mouth. "We were sending her money the whole time. I just feel like everybody needs a college education now."

Four weeks after Ms. Nelms had enrolled at ASU, her father said he learned of her involvement with The Way. "She was a little homesick, a little lonesome," he said. "I was stupid on it. Thanksgiving is when I found out that it was serious. I asked her not to go back with that group."

At Christmas, he purchased the young woman a brand-new $9,800 car, registering it in his name and telling her that she could have it on the condition that she steer clear of the group. Nelms finished his third cigarette. His expensive gift to his little girl didn't change a thing.

"The group was using the car—she was walking where she needed to go. It was what she felt she was supposed to do. She pawned her class ring; I went and got that back." A Boone Baptist Student Union representative called Nelms after spring semester had begun, informing him that his daughter had not attended classes in three weeks. It was ultimately the denomination of Nelms's faith that saved his daughter from the jaws of The Way International.

Finally, it became distinctly apparent that she would not be continuing her education, so when Nelms came up to help her pack her clothes in her dorm room, there was company—Way members. "They were standing there, looking at me, calling me 'kidnapper.' I wasn't afraid, a little ill…I really wasn't ill," Nelms said. "I'm going to put it like this—I didn't listen to them. We talked to a lady [in Castalia] as far as counseling, talked to a minister, and long that night, sometime around one or two o'clock, that's when she took the car and came back up here. I told her, 'Don't take the car.'"

She should have taken his advice, or maybe it was a good thing that she broke the law. Upon Nelms's request, Franklin County Sheriff's Department authorities drew up warrants for Ms. Karen Nelms and her arrest on the charge of felonious automobile larceny, and a Boone detective served them on her outside the Way apartment in Boone. The detective was Bob Kennedy.

All this time, Nelms had hired a private detective to trail his daughter. One of the hardest things a parent might have to do with a child is to put the law on his or her progeny. It's the ultimate parental right of custody and persuasion.

"They released her to my custody, and she refused to go with me, of course. After talking with me, I did get her to go with me," Nelms said. "She told me that she was afraid to go."

She was about to visit Iowa for the first time in her life. Two of the deprogrammers were women, one of whom was a psychiatrist, he said, and another counselor was a former Way member himself. Nelms said that he was present for about 95 percent of the week, which he said was punctuated by late-night sessions and proper meals but not contact with the outside world.

Nelms felt that the spot in Iowa was "safe" from the Boone group. "She stayed five days, made four phone calls while she was there," he said. Two calls were made to the Pizza Hut in Boone, where she had worked, and two were made to her home in Castalia, he said.

Ms. Nelms later admitted that someone had given her assistance so she could travel back to Boone. For six days, Nelms said, he didn't know where she was until she called him. "She told me how much she loved me," said Nelms. I asked the guy if he loved his daughter.

"Would you spend $20,000, and that's how much I spent, would that mean I loved her or not? I didn't have it. My friends have taken care of all my farming, my chicken houses. Anyway, they could help me, they have helped me, and they have helped me financially."

Officer Bob Kennedy was in the courtroom during that trial. I was really sad to hear about Bob Kennedy's death. He was such a great guy and a super cop. Everybody liked him. Bob Kennedy is still looking for marijuana in the North Carolina mountain skies.

Following is the cross-examination of Karen Nelms by the prosecutor when one Way member was tried for breaking into a cigarette machine at a Japanese restaurant:

Q. *"Now, you say you were a student at one time?"*
A. *"Yes, sir."*
Q. *"When did you leave school?"*
A. *"Last semester; well, I finished one semester."*
Q. *"Why did you leave, ma'am?"*
A. *"I didn't like it. School wasn't for me."*
Q. *"Why didn't you like it?"*
A. *"I just don't like to study."*
Q. *"Why?"*
A. *"Because of my parents."*

Q. *"Because of your parents?"*
A. *"Yes, they wanted me to go."*
Q. *"How far had you gone in school?"*
A. *"One semester."*
Q. *"One semester."*
A. *"Uh huh."*
Q. *"How did you get involved in The Way?"*
A. *"I met them watching TV, and they asked me if I wanted to come to a fellowship, and I agreed."*
Q. *"And you work at the Pizza Hut now?"*
A. *"Yes, sir."*
Q. *"Do you contribute your wages to The Way?"*
A. *"Yes, sir. Not my wages, a percent."*
Q. *"What percent?"*
A. *"Ten percent or what I have. What I can give of that."*
Q. *"Ten percent?"*
A. *"Yes, sir."*

Word Over the World (WOW) ambassadors preached just that message: "The Word Over the World." The crux of The Way's mission was Wierwille's Power for Abundant Living course.

In the fall of 1975, the new leader said that he had entered the Way College of Emporia to start the second Way Corps training locale.

"I really feel it's a totalistic group," Priscilla Coates, director of the Citizens Freedom Foundation in Hannacroix, New York, told me. The anti-cult agency had fifty-five affiliates in thirty-one states, including North Carolina, with offices in Greensboro and Raleigh. "Whoever leads The Way, leads it with total control," she said. "It's his way—or no way."

The most chilling aspect of Way activities is its paramilitary weapons training, she said, which was publicized after people heard of a National Guard weapons course being taken by Way college students in New Knoxville. There has never been anything like teaching Jesus with as strong a brand of *pow-pow* as we see today.

"We don't have it anymore," said another Way spokesperson. Is there mind control and brainwashing in The Way? "My answer to that would simply be come for yourself and make your own judgment," said one spokesman.

As The Way's official public relations officer, a woman addressed the accusation of brainwashing. "The charge of brainwashing is basically introduced to cause confusion and suspicion," she said. "Nobody can pin down what it is that they think we are doing because it doesn't exist. Unfortunately, we have a number of these kinds of complaints. Sometimes parents are victims of a fast-talking deprogrammer who is trying to make his commission like a salesman does. It is kidnapping and therefore illegal." I recall the "No Soliciting" sign on our door and the unrelenting line of salesmen, church doughnut pitch-children and other hawkers who broke the city's peddler law daily and forced me to do a story on the law.

Concerning the David Michael Reilly case—in which a member of the local group was charged with breaking into a Japanese steakhouse he worked at and stealing money out of a vandalized cigarette machine—she said, "My major concern is what he did is not a reflection of what our organization teaches." She continued: "We do not support kidnapping or holding a person against their will."

Ms. Coates of CFF said that the thing that had upset her the most about The Way hit her as she was reading one day. A writer wrote that Wierwille's hometown is only forty-seven miles from Lynn, Indiana—the birthplace of Reverend Jim Jones, who led more than nine hundred cankered souls to suicide in Jonestown. God knows what went on in Iowa City, Iowa, where our crying North Carolina farmer sent $20,000 of plow money to get his daughter deprogrammed, but what happened afterward was a tragedy. As Henry David Thoreau said, "Heaven is under our feet as well as over our heads."

Freedom of religion is a constitutional right respected by Reverend David Long of First Presbyterian Church in Boone. To find a clear, level-headed response and explanation of cult groups, I figured that the reasonable place to start was with a Protestant officiant.

"We have to allow and protect, under the law, a group like The Way," Long said. "I'd describe it as a very dangerous cult by what I know and what I've read—it's very dangerous. They accept the scriptures, but they vary from them. Pretty soon, they have you off out here. The church doesn't have all the truth about the scriptures."

Long described the person susceptible to a cult: "The person who has biblical or religious or Christian training, the person who has a church background, the person who is not the most popular person, but who needs approval of friends…a rather strict upbringing, a so-called sheltered life, a person who is lonely, lonely from family, lonely from friends, and they really lack a personal relationship with God." Later, when I asked Long about speaking in tongues and exorcism, he said that he saw an exorcism in Africa and believed that one could speak in tongues.

A North Carolina Way director in Greenville, North Carolina, told me, "One man's cult is another man's religion, and one man's religion is another man's cult.

Ms. Nelms asked me to print that she loves her parents and has not tried to do anything to hurt them. The next time I saw her she was with Edwards in our front office, buying a classified ad for the sale of a $175 flute.

The Nelmses' experience is not new in North Carolina. "No, it's not the first case I know of," said an anti-cult spokesman. "They are in every state."

Colonization of Way groups evolved into a network encompassing all fifty states and fifty foreign countries since Wierwille, born in 1917, quit his ministry at United Church of Christ in Van Wert, Ohio, to inoculate his own herd. He studied at Mission House College, Moody Bible Institute, the University of Chicago Divinity School, getting his masters of theology from Princeton Theological Seminary and his doctorate from Pike's Peak Seminary, an alleged "degree mill."

Boone Way fellowship meetings were held at 8:00 p.m. every Tuesday and Friday night, so on April 29, before a spokesman had invited me to attend, I went with my cousin, Jeff, who lives forty-five miles away in Newton. He's husky like me, and we look and feel like brothers. I asked him to go, and he was hesitant, but agreed when it looked like we would.

Twig leader Pat Yaconis preached out of the books of Acts and Ephesians, talking about change and how those who persecute might be converted. It was a nice house on a respectable street above the Flick theater. Prayers were uttered, and a reed horn of plenty was passed around, so I gave Wierwille a buck—didn't even ask for compensation at work (there are a lot of invisible costs for journalists). Karen Nelms had been contributing 10 percent of her waitress money to the group. I'm just not a 10 percenter at heart. One of my stories quoted estimated Way assets at $10 million or near that amount.

I thought I'd melt from embarrassment when we started singing some corny oldie-but-goldies from the *Sing Along The Way* songbook, but everyone else chimed in with laughs and cheer. "Again, what you saw is not different from anything else we do," The Way spokesman reminded me later. The merriment subsided into a serious conversation when I told them I was a news reporter. Somber indeed.

Yaconis said that he'd have to refer questions to New Knoxville, but he did say, "David [Reilly] is not guilty."

Mark Edwards, sitting next to Way member Karen Nelms, said that the group had contacted the FBI in Hickory to report that the group was being railroaded, but no assistance was given.

On New Year's Eve, David Michael Reilly, twenty-three, of Methuen, Massachusetts, found himself facing charges of felonious breaking and entering and larceny because of an incident in November 1982 at a Japanese steakhouse where he worked. A vandalized cigarette machine was smashed, and money was stolen. Boone Police Department officers had arrested him at the twig's $450-a-month home, charging that he had stolen $6,767 from the restaurant on Saturday, November 21. More than $5,000 damage was sustained at the location of our newspaper's company Christmas party, a Japanese restaurant where the showboat chefs feigned translation difficulties until they had captured a fair maiden customer following the flaming shrimp ritual and the miracle of catching a yellow rind of lemon behind the back on the second or third try.

The company safe was found opened on the lobby floor.

After Way member David Michael Reilly was taken by the Boone Police Department and went to court, Henry Upchurch of Sugar Grove, eight miles from Boone near Vilas, made his $10,000 bond. Reilly received a three-year sentence. After a Watauga County jury deliberated for about four hours on April 15 before convicting Reilly, he got a three-year active sentence.

During his trial, Reilly's attorney argued fiercely when the judge allowed the prosecutor's questioning to ramble way out of bounds into The Way's financial transactions and to a crazy little thing called deprogramming. A Boone detective testified that Reilly had protested when he was arrested and that during questioning the suspect stated that "he had no damned business around that cigarette machine."

Prints found on the cigarette machine were "fresh," the officer testified, having been applied within forty-eight hours of the break-in. The prints were identified as Reilly's. "He has no prior record, to my knowledge," he said. "A vendor said that when he checked his machine after the crime, cigarettes were missing, but no money had been swiped. A Makoto's assistant manager testified that the defendant, a former morning janitor, had been relieved of his duties over a week before the theft because he had missed a day of work."

"I thought it was my day off," Reilly testified later. He and other Way members were sworn in together, with their hands placed squarely on Bibles. Reilly said that he had been bowling and watching TV.

Federal Bureau of Investigation special agent Johnny Turner told me that his department had assisted former Boone police chief Clyde Tester and his staff in the Reilly investigation.

Nelms lighted his fifth cigarette, and Bob Kennedy and I listened as the room began to get pretty smoky. He said that when he would drive to Boone to see his daughter, Way members were always with her and would watch them until the end of the visits.

A North Carolina State Bureau of Investigation (SBI) agent told me that there was no ongoing investigation of The Way, but he referred to information in an article in the *Raleigh News & Observer* published on April 6, 1981. The story reported on ex-Way member and North Carolina State University Wolfpack student David Richard's disillusionment with one of the ten fellowships in the Raleigh area in the fall of 1973 and his charges of mind control, fraternity-joke hazing, sleep deprivation and malnourishment.

Another Way member in Boone, Susannah Reece, testified in the Reilly trial. "Jesus Christ is the Son of God," she said under oath, adding that she stays in the group of her own free will. Her mother, Mary Reece, told me later that after reading some Way documents her daughter brought home one weekend, she believed that the Way doctrines are not too kosher and were definitely unlike the preachings of the family's worship at Pine Log Baptist Church. "Great name," Susannah had written in the margin.

Susannah testified that she had met Way member Mark Edward in August and that she went to a meeting because she was interested in what the group had to say. "They were really excited about being alive, and I wanted to know how to be that way," she said. "They smile a lot."

Reilly explained how he had met other Way members. "We went to this thing called the Rock of Ages; it's this thing like a Christian gathering," he said. He and his new friends then moved to Hickory and on to Boone, forty-five miles away. He said that he had signed an application to become a Word Over the World (WOW) ambassador. All local twig group money now goes to Way treasurer Howard Allen, according to Reilly.

Ms. Nelms later spent a weekend at home with her family. Her father drove her back to Boone, as he promised he would. This was in the 1980s. Are cult members evil? Can people speak in tongues? Superstition abounds in the Tar Heel State.

In Fayetteville, a conjuring man was feared, but in town they made money in practice. One woman paid $5 to the man to cast a spell on a man who went out with her daughter.

"The conjure man had put the hair of a horse's tail, two needles, gunpowder and a small rock into a bag and buried it under the doorstep of the man he was throwing." The man also allegedly sold magical handkerchiefs that cured any pain.

Everyone from Boone to Winston-Salem has heard of the Little Red Man at Old Salem in the Brothers House. He was Andreas Kremser, who died and was buried in "God's Acre." Born March 7, 1753, in Pennsylvania, he came to North Carolina in October 1766 to work as a shoemaker. He moved to Salem on February 6, 1772. He was helping excavate the cellar, and he was covered by falling earth. The doctor opened his arm's vein, and he died at about 2:00 a.m.

Later, people would hear taps of a shoemaker hammer.

"There's Kremser!" workers would say. Some would see his red cap.

One child saw a little man beckoning her with his finger. Then one day a visiting preacher ordered Kremser to leave the premises with an exorcism.

The money from the Boone restaurant was never returned or recovered. Bob Kennedy's friends still remember his work in law enforcement and his courage, faith and dignity. A lawman's work is never done. If you look to the heavens, you may have to squint a little, but you may see that plane in the sky on its eternal pursuit of protecting the peace and serving the public.

GHOSTS OF THE DURHAM FAMILY

Perpetually freezing, the winter wind swirls white clouds of snow, muting the thuds and muzzling the muffled screams from within a warm home to a family of three—a structure about to become an empty, lifeless dwelling, only a house with a tub of running water. There were three bodies that night in 1972, submerged, their souls searching for justice until their killers get what they deserve.

Driving to Boone, North Carolina, one day in our black Toyota Corolla, I passed the *Watauga Democrat*'s former location on Main Street and headed out to the hilly side of town toward Tennessee. You take a left to reach the sheriff's department, which is situated across from a rustic rural church.

You also take a left to swing down the NC 105 extension, a highway I used to get to many a party when I was living in Boone as a student and a reporter at the *Watauga Democrat* newspaper. I was headed to the old Durham house, and little did I know that I'd be asked to come on inside and sit a spell.

Never before had I believed in ghosts. It's just superstitious fantasy, a self-inflicted fear on top of our normal daily neuroses and religious transgressions. We used to visit graveyards in high school in order to scare the mess out of girls so they would rush into our arms in the cool midnight air of fall. There is a certain smell to death, a sweet smell, which I experienced after my grandfather died. It was in his hospital room. I never wanted to smell that smell again.

At night, when you go to bed, you pull the sheets up, and as a child you wonder what is under your bed, what is making those weird noises under

The home where members of the Durham family were brutally murdered is unassuming, located on Townsend Road outside of Boone. Ghosts have been seen and heard in this house. *Photo by Tim Bullard.*

the bed or what is scratching at the window. My most frightening nightmare was a shadow at the door, beyond the gauzed curtains, as the door opens to loud, demon-like chuckling. I never believed in ghosts until I visited the home outside of Boone where a sickening crime took place two years before Nixon resigned.

A Boone, North Carolina woman says that her home is haunted, and whether you believe in ghosts or not, there may be some truth to her story—that is, if spirits give clues.

Karen Coffey Wood said one morning, "I've lived here since 1997." She was born in Boone. Her father, Harold, has operated the Hilltop Drive-In outside of town for thirty-seven years, and her coffee was hot and tasty. He was working that night, the night the Durhams were slayed.

Wood said that her father saw the cop cars go by as he was cleaning in the restaurant. He had the front door open, and it was quiet outside. He was mopping and cleaning. The Durham family had often come into the restaurant to eat. He said that they were really nice people. They were murdered that night: a mom, dad and son, a student at Appalachian State. The Watauga County Sheriff's Department is taking a new look into the case.

"He remembers Mr. Durham, the son and the wife," she said. "Students a few years ago were doing a paper on the murder. They wanted to come in the house step-by-step and take pictures where the bodies were. We let them come in. They were trying to solve the mystery, but I don't think they ever solved it."

"I know there are creaks in an old house," she continued. "I know when I am sitting in the den, my bedroom, the master bedroom, is right above the den upstairs. So when I am sitting in the den, I can hear footsteps in my room." Her boy was always asleep when this happened.

Then, sometimes, I sleep upstairs by myself. At night I can feel something in the room, like a presence. Then I will wake up in the middle of the night, and my TV is on, and I'll turn it off. I'll go back to sleep, and it will come back on, so I'll just unplug it.

Then sometimes I'll be in my room, and the channels will keep flipping, and it will stop on the news or something. I'll say, "Okay, that's fine, Mr. Durham. We'll watch the news." The channels will start flipping again. My son, his room is finished in the basement. He said his stereo will come on sometimes wide open, and it will go back down. My daughter keeps telling me there is a man in her room.

Her room is right across from the bathroom, where the bodies were found. She said, "There's a man standing behind my door." I say, "Oh, it's probably a ghost. It won't hurt you." Then she will smile. She was home one day, and she called me and said, "Mom! There's a lady on the couch in the living room." I said, "What is she doing?" She said, "She's looking at the clock and the fireplace." I said, "Well don't be scared, it's probably a ghost."

The lady vanished.

"I hear footsteps running up and down the steps sometimes," she said. "I'm not afraid of them. I don't feel like it's a scary presence. I do feel something. I believe there are spirits that are lost. I do believe in them. When I'm laying down in my bed, I can feel someone laying there beside me, and there is no one there. It's the same exact bathtub still." The address is 187 Clyde Townsend Road, and 187 is the police code for homicide.

In 1972, three family members were murdered in their home off Clyde Townsend Road, and retired SBI agent Charles Whitman and other lawmen are helping the Watauga County Sheriff's Department with a fresh look at the unsolved mystery of the Durham family murders, an unsolved triple homicide from February 3, 1972.

Boone native Rufus Edmisten was an aide and chief counsel to U.S. Senator Sam Ervin (D-NC) from 1964 to 1974 and was also the deputy chief counsel on the Senate Watergate Committee. You would always see him in the background during the televised hearings with his trademark pipe. He was secretary of state from 1989 to 1996. Now he is a partner with the Edmisten & Webb law firm practicing civil law.

"Obviously, the killings occurred before I became attorney general in 1974," said Edmisten. "But almost immediately when I became attorney general, I knew about it when I was with Senator Ervin. I kept hearing about it, and people talked with me about it. I talked to the sheriff about it. I talked to the Boone police chief, Clyde Tester, about it, because it was home, my hometown. It made all these detective magazines."

He continued:

> It made the national news et cetera, and then I became attorney general, and there was a renewed interest to it from lots of people from Boone, so I said this case looks to me like it is ripe for reopening. I spent more personal time on this case than probably any other case in the department. Every time I would fly anywhere near Boone, the Durhams would be there, Mr. and Mrs. Durham, the mother and father of Bryce Durham, the deceased father.
>
> They'd tell me that before they died, they wanted this case solved because it was the most heartbreaking thing in the world for them. Obviously it was their son, his wife and their grandson, Bobby.

The North Carolina State Bureau of Investigation helped out tremendously on the case, according to Edmisten:

Oh absolutely. Absolutely. The State Bureau of Investigation was in on it from the beginning. For one, they had been on the investigation from the beginning, and when I reopened it, I had thousands of hours I spent on the case, going over old leads, checking out this and that. This is one of the most mysterious cases in our entire history. The Durham case is so intriguing. Almost everybody is a suspect. All the theories in the world started piling up on that, the military. When something like that happens, you have to be close to law enforcement to know every theory known to mankind will pop up. You go over it over and over again, and it defies anything I've ever encountered before in law enforcement because nothing ever came up after going over it over and over and over again.

The conspiracy theories included the military, he said, and drugs. "It goes on and on and on. I could talk for twenty hours about that case. The house is out on 105," he said. John Butts, head of the North Carolina Chief Medical Examiner's Office, said that all records on crimes before 1976 had been

Former North Carolina attorney general Rufus Edmisten, *left*, a Boone native, tried to solve the Durham murders case. Here he was with Hart Hodges, Governor Luther H. Hodges's grandson, sticking Grandfather Mountain bumper stickers on a car in the parking lot of Grandfather Mountain in 1969. *Courtesy of Hugh Morton Collection of Photographs & Films, Wilson Library, North Carolina Collection Photographic Archives, University of North Carolina–Chapel Hill.*

destroyed. "Who you need to talk to is Charles Whitman," said Edmisten. "He's been retired a long time. Back when I reopened the case, I put Charlie Whitman on it." Edmisten reopened the case about 1982.

Will it ever be solved? "Well I'll tell you this. It will be an eternal mystery," Edmisten said. "Obviously they knew how to kill people because they hogtied them. They drowned them. There was some sinister motive other than just people walking off the street because it was a cold, wintery, blustery night. You know, they had to go to great lengths and great trouble to do it."

Were the culprits drug-addled? "I do not believe so. I've always believed that this was a contract killing," he said. "It was not a drug-addled person because, as I recall, they were all three hogtied in military fashion, submerged in the bathtub. There had to be a number of people there to do it. It's one of the great mysteries of North Carolina…I have my doubts when one goes that long unsolved with that much notoriety and publicity, I doubt it will be solved."

What did it feel like to be on the Watergate team with Ervin? "I'm looking now at the original subpoena that I served on Richard Nixon for the tapes. It was one of the most exciting times in American history. The whole world was clutched on what was happening on the Watergate, and there I was right in the middle of it, a young boy from Boone, North Carolina. I was very honored. Every day had some kind of shock and awe."

Whitman talked about the case, adding that the chief investigator of the Wilkes County Sheriff's Department also worked on the case. That man, Steve Cabe, has died, as has former Watauga County sheriff Ward Carroll, who worked the case, but I talked to Ward right before he died.

Whitman recalled what he was doing the day of the crime. "Before I got the call, as I remember that day, the SBI is divided into districts. Our district held a meeting that day. I got the call about eleven o'clock p.m. I'm sure you can appreciate this," he said. "I may have been in bed five minutes when the phone rang. At that time, there was an agent here by the name of Wallace Hardwick. He responded and called me, and I in turn called our mobile crime lab and got him on the way here."

"So, essentially, I think it was maybe two or three days later I got home, just more or less to change clothes, and then went right straight back. I may have laid down and closed my eyes for a few minutes. Other than that, I got there at the house midnight-ish, a few minutes before. It's probably in the report exactly what time."

Whitman described the weather. "Boone winter. It started snowing at about three o'clock that afternoon, and it got worse, and it got worse, and it got worse," he said. "At nine o'clock that night, there was a good three inches of snow on the ground. It was still coming down fiercely. The winds were blowing and howling. I doubt seriously the next-door neighbor could have heard anything going on. The wind was really howling…Had there been any shoe tracks or car tracks, they would have been covered up almost immediately."

February 3, 1972, is a day that he will never forget, and he recalls the events of this homicide with calculated memory untouched by time, narrating the events without hesitation because he has told it many times. It was the day the Winter Olympics had started in Japan.

"It was a Thursday night," Whitman recalled of the murders. "Of course, the pivotal thing was the three bodies in the bathtub. If you come in the front door, and I think that's the door I came in, that's almost the first thing you would see after taking a couple of steps in; you see the bodies headfirst into the bathtub." The victims were clothed, he said.

"Bobby and Mrs. Durham did not have their shoes on. However, Bobby's shoes were laced up Oxfords, and Mrs. Durham's, at the time we called them fashion boots. They came up to the knee and zipped. Mrs. Durham's fashion boots and Bobby's shoes were neatly placed inside the front door," he said. "That was indicative of somebody coming in with snow on them. I examined the under soles, and both of them were still damp. Now Mr. Durham had been wearing totes. It's just a rubber pull-on outer boot. He still had on his dress Oxfords; however, the totes were upstairs in the master bedroom, which would indicate that Mr. Durham got upstairs."

"In addition to his totes, his overcoat was also upstairs, and it was just more or less draped over the edge of the closet door. So Mr. Durham got upstairs. We would have to assume that he got back downstairs. It would be a guess as to whether he was forced downstairs or if things had not started to happen when he came back downstairs," he continued. "Mr. Durham was in the middle. Bobby was closest to the drain and Mrs. Durham was at the far end, Virginia. I did not know them. They had only lived in Boone about eighteen months. They came here from Mount Airy."

Durham was supposedly going to go into the auto business in Boone with an unknown partner. "For some unknown reason, and I don't know, the partner backed out, leaving Mr. Durham with the entire load, if you will. I don't recall that his name ever surfaced. In Mount Airy, Mr. Durham was in the auto loan business. There was an agent living in Mount Airy, and he was assigned, and later on other agents were assigned to just look into things around Mount Airy trying to establish a motive."

Was there more than one intruder? "Well, I think it would be safe to assume that it would require several people, because we're talking about two adults and one muscular nineteen-year-old boy. He was already at ASU. She helped out at the Buick dealership. Her nose was bloodied, and there was a small blood pattern in the den. This was on shag carpet." That spot is where the apparition had been seen.

Is there any DNA evidence from the crime? "No, because the only blood was hers. There was no other unidentified blood in the house," he said. "There was no unidentified hair that I recall."

When told that Edmisten still thinks that it was a contract killing, he responded, "That would fit as well as anything. If there was a contract, you've got to ask yourself, why an entire family? I can tell you that Bobby was the first one to go in the tub. I can tell you that Mr. Durham was the second one to go in the tub, and Mrs. Durham was at the far end."

He characterized the number of hours spent on the case. "There would be no way. We even had the director, Charles Dunn, here to look this over. We looked into the possibility that this was a house burglary gang, and there was a team of SBI agents moved into Wilkes County because at that time there were one or two house burglary gangs operating," he said. "We had no reason, plausible reason, to think that they may have been involved, but it was one of those things that you had to eliminate. However, nothing was turned up there. I think there were six agents on it for about a year."

Did a military group do it? "Again, it's sort of like with the house burglary people. At the time that this happened, there was a detachment of Green Berets going through ski training at Appalachian Ski Mountain between here and Blowing Rock. In fact, that's where Mr. Durham and the Rotary Club met that night."

"The detachment of Green Berets was supposed to give the Rotary Club a demonstration of their skiing ability," he continued. "However, keep in mind that it started snowing about three o'clock that afternoon, and it got worse and worse and worse. So they could not give this demonstration. Mr. Durham they normally met at the Holiday Inn, but on this particular night they met at the ski mountain."

"They got over their meeting about 8:15 p.m., and Mr. Durham was part of what I would call a loose caravan of other Rotarians who were leaving about the same time," he said. "I forgot his name, but one of the Rotarians followed Mr. Durham all the way to the Buick place. You know where Perkinsville is? Just before you get to Perkinsville is where you would come around 105 Bypass and turn right on 421 like you're going toward

Perkinsville. When you make that right turn, you go two hundred to three hundred yards, and there was a building on the right, Modern Buick. That was what Mr. Durham ran."

Durham pulled in there at 8:30 p.m., Whitman said.

That afternoon, because of the snow, he asked one of his salesmen to gas up a Jimmy, a four-wheel drive. It was one of four that just came in that afternoon or the day before. The salesman gassed it up because Mr. Durham didn't feel like his regular car would make it up that hill. So when Mr. Durham came back, it is my contention that he came to pick up his wife. At about six o'clock or a few minutes after, and I don't know who called whom, the lawyer called Mrs. Durham about a tax matter. She made the comment to this attorney that, "I've got fourteen hours of work staring me in the face."

So we feel that she stayed at the Buick place until Mr. Durham came and picked her up. We know that almost straight up and down that they arrived home at around nine o'clock. We also know that they did not make the night deposit because it was on the dining room table with money in it. "Weird" is one word, yes.

We also feel like that Bobby was there also. Both his car and the Durham car that they would normally drive were both in the parking area of Modern Buick. Now there was no snow under Mr. Durham's car, so we feel it had not been moved. There was some snow under Bobby's car, but not a great deal. Now you know where Wal-Mart is? If you remember Rose's was there.

We've got Bobby talking to a friend at about 7:30 p.m. And she says that she's reasonably sure that he had just come in because the snow in his hair had not melted. We still feel that Bobby was at the Buick place waiting on his daddy.

Who found the bodies? "We've got a daughter," he said. "Her name was Ginny (Sue). She had recently married this guy by the name of Troy Hall, and they lived near the A&P. The backstreet, there was a Baptist church and as you go on past there, there was a trailer park on your left. This is where Jenny and her husband lived, two miles from where her parents lived."

"What we've got here is the husband, Troy Hall, supposedly left the trailer about 5:00 p.m., give or take, went to the library and studied," he said. "According to her, he came back about five minutes till 10:00 p.m. He wanted to watch the Winter Olympics. She says that he was coming in about the time that they were playing the theme song for the Winter Olympics. They watched television for ten to fifteen minutes, and the television went on the blink," he said. Then they put on music. "Somewhere around 10:15 p.m. the telephone rang. Troy answered it, and Jenny hears him say, 'Virginia, is that you?' And he came back and made the comment, 'Would your mother play a trick on us?' They tried to call back and got a busy signal."

The call, he said, is a clue.

Detectives have to sift out fact from fiction, and sometimes there is a gray area. "Just about everything brought to our attention was purely speculative," Whitman said. "For example I told you about the marines here. We had some people tell us that that was the way the Green Berets killed people in Vietnam." The victims had been strangled with a rope, he added.

"It was just a sash rope. It's about a quarter to a half-inch in diameter, and it's woven cotton strands," he said. "This was found on Mr. Durham's neck loosely. It was about six feet long with a large rope tied in one end. Now Mrs. Durham showed evidence of strangulation. Mr. Durham did, and Bobby did. Mrs. Durham was already dead when she was placed in the tub, and she was the last one to go in. So there are just so many things. Could this have happened? Could that have happened? Bobby and Mr. Durham showed evidence of drowning as well as strangulation."

How would he characterize this type of killing? "I don't know that I have ever experienced one of that magnitude. Certainly not in this part of the country," he said. Both adults were about fifty.

What about the killers? "In 1982 or '83, I took the file to the FBI's profiler, not because I was involved in this case, but the profiler looked over the case, and we spent a total of twelve hours with him," he said. "Now I say this objectively, he says that 'we do not spend normally more than two hours on a case.' But he said, 'This case not only intrigues me, but I do not know if I have ever seen one as well put-together as far as documentation.' That made us feel pretty good."

"The main thing that I remember the profiler saying was that the perpetrator probably felt comfortable in the house," Whitman said. "I'm not sure how to evaluate that. If you're dealing with total strangers like in a contract killing, perhaps the perpetrator would feel comfortable because he is dealing with strangers. Here again this is speculation," he said.

After the telephone call, he talked about what happened. "It was local, so there would be no telephone record. They decided to go over to the house. Here again, there is speculation," he said. "But this was around 10:15 p.m. Keep in mind, Troy had just come in at ten o'clock. But they could not get

This is the final resting place of Virginia Church Durham, who was from Wilkes County. *Photo by Tim Bullard.*

their car started. In talking to the daughter, I talked to her with deep interest about how the car sounded. She said, 'It just clicked.' That can mean several things, but primarily a dead battery. That would be my opinion."

"So they go down to a guy who lived two trailers down from them, a manager. Cecil Small was his name. He was sort of the manager of the trailer park, and he was also a private detective. So they come down and get Cecil to drive them over to the Durham house. This is approximately two miles. As you go out 105 like you're going to Linville, you go out and turn right and that brings you out to the bypass and 421. The house is on that road," he said. "It was on 105 Bypass. The house is still there. It's among eight or ten houses. It's up on a hill. It was a two-story house. At any rate, they either tried or felt like they could not drive up to the house because of the snow. So Troy and Cecil Small leave Ginny in the car, and they walk up to the house."

"They walk around the house, look in. The spring that holds down one of these doors. It malfunctions sometimes," he said. "It had come loose, and it had come up about eighteen inches. This is how they got into the house. From the garage, that took them into the den. From the den, you can go to the left and go into the living room or you can go to the right and go down a hall to the kitchen and also to the living room."

"There is a telephone in the kitchen. It had been jerked out of the wall. It has a cradle and an earpiece and a coiled cord," he said. "It had been jerked out where the coiled cord goes into the base. Now keep in mind that supposedly Mrs. Durham called her son-in-law or daughter or whichever. This is why when they tried to call back they got a busy signal, allegedly."

"They, Troy and Cecil Small, Cecil goes to the left, and he has to pass the bathroom, and he looks in the bathroom, and there they are," he said. "According to Cecil, he thought he heard something, and he got Troy and got out of there. They go back to the car. This is the thing that makes it so peculiar. They leave, but they got stuck in the snow. I asked Cecil, 'What were you going to do?' He said, 'I was just going to get away from there.' So since they couldn't get away from there, they go to an apartment right close by and make a telephone call from then which was at 10:50 p.m." Small got stuck in the snow, he said.

There was a fire there a year ago with three girls burned to death, Whitman said. "This apartment complex is where Troy and Cecil Small went to make the telephone call. The Jimmy was seen coming off a residential area at 10:30 p.m. They almost ran the driver off the road. This guy he followed them on out to the main 105 where you would turn right, which he did, to Linville. He said the car turned left going back toward Boone, the Jimmy. It turned left like coming back toward Boone."

"He got home at 10:30 p.m., the guy who turned right," he said. "About the first road you could turn left on, the Jimmy was found abandoned, but it was in a ditch. This is a four-wheel drive. There was no indication that it slid into the ditch. It was just there with the lights on and the motor running." That is 2.2 miles from the scene of the crime.

"Speculation. Speculation. Speculation. Keep in mind the telephone call," he said. "Why did the perpetrators need the Durham Jimmy to get away from there? I don't know. I do not know; however, we can account for every vehicle that went up that road that night during this critical period of time. We know the Durhams got home about exactly nine o'clock."

Whitman said the father and son both showed evidence of strangulation and drowning.

Who did it? "I haven't the slightest idea," said Whitman.

Will it ever be solved? "The FBI profiler, another thing he told us was the longer the perpetrator can go without confessing to anybody the easier it becomes, and finally it's like you've got an out-of-body experience that there is somebody else doing this. Now this has been since February 1972." He laughs.

Are the killers still alive? "If I could satisfy myself as to why. We know how. That's no problem. We know when. That's no problem. But personally, I don't know why. There are so many things. Was the son involved in any kind of dope traffic? Negative. Was Mr. Durham involved in something in Mount Airy? Negative. Everything that we have done has come up negative, although we had a confession…I thought you would perk up on that," he said. "It was another one of those dead ends. He confessed to it. His cell mate at Central Prison backed him up. There was one slight problem. He said he shot him. Then there was another slight problem. He was in prison when it happened. This is the thing. You've got to check it out. It was another one of those dead ends."

What about deathbed confessions? "I've had one or two in my career. That could happen. But whoever it is has kept it inside since 1972," he said. "If I knew why, was it a contract killing? If so, who was the main person they were interested in? The house was made to look like it had been ransacked, all the drawers pulled out, the contents dumped on the floor. When you first come in, things are chaotic. It just has the appearance of a burglary. But when you stand back and sort of look at it with an experienced eye, if you will, the whole thing was staged. Now I don't know why."

"Why was it necessary to go to all this trouble? Now if it was going to be a contract killing, it would seem that you would go in and bang-bang and strangle," he said. "You go in and do the job and then you leave. I have found this to be significant. There was not one drop of water on the floor outside the tub, which means none of them floundered around or resisted a great deal after they went in the tub."

(Whenever I write about this case, I feel a cool sensation and a feeling I am not alone. The Durhams have made their presence known to me since I started covering this triple homicide as a journalist. I used to want to see someone brought to justice. Now I want to scare the suspects, to make it harder to sleep at night. When you can do that, you've done your job as a writer. Once the Hickory Police Department called me to cover a perp walk of a cocaine suspect, but I had forgotten to load my camera with film, so I started clicking anyway as the person shielded his face. Three ghosts watch me now.)

Whitman said that Durham had repossessed cars in his career. "If the FBI profiler was correct, what type of person would be in a comfortable atmosphere when three people were being murdered at the time?"

If authorities learned who did it, could the persons be prosecuted? "There is no time limit on murder," said the former agent. "It could be fifty years from now. It doesn't make any difference. Obviously, time clouds people's minds and their recollections. I've had several meetings with Sheriff L.D. Hagaman up here about this case," he said. "We have met with some of the other investigators, most of whom, like myself, are retired, but they still have an interest, like Sheriff Ward Carroll, who was sheriff at that time. I see him occasionally. Of course, this is one of the first things that he brings up. The people who lived here at that time and know that I worked on that case—this is one of the first things they bring up. Usually it's before they say, 'Hello. How are you?' So the case is still alive, and as I said, it may take fifty years. The rope that was around Mr. Durham's neck is still accounted for. There are still pictures that could be introduced. It very definitely is not dead and can be prosecuted at any time."

Could DNA come from the rope? "There was no indication that there was anything on it. There's no blood trail or body fluids," he said. "DNA is a good thing. I just saw in the paper this morning that some guy was released after eighteen years because somebody else's DNA was on the victim's undergarments. DNA is sort of like fingerprints. You find a fingerprint at the scene of a crime, that fingerprint is of no value until you find somebody to match it with."

What about the new sheriff and his department? "Len Hagaman and I go back many years. I personally think he is doing a crackup job as sheriff. He is certainly knowledgeable," he said. "This case was one of the first things that he jumped on after becoming sheriff. We had a meeting, some other investigators like myself. We spent probably one whole afternoon going over 'What do you remember?' He's interested even though this case is as old as it is. There's not another one around, a triple murder, like that around here?"

Just who was Baxter Bryce Durham? To learn more about this man, you have to look at the certificate of death from the Medical Examiner's Office at the North Carolina State Board of Health Office of Vital Statistics in Raleigh—book no. 59, page 50. The date of death is listed as February 3, 1972, in Watauga County, Route 3, outside the city limits of Boone. He was married, with a Social Security number of 238-20-2213.

Baxter Bryce Durham was the owner of an auto dealership, according to the certificate, and his father's name was Coy Durham. His mother's name was listed as Collie Crabb Durham. His daughter is listed as Mrs. Ginny (Sue) D. Hall of 57 Greenway Village, Boone.

Baxter Bryce Durham sold cars for a living before his life was ended, along with that of his family, in 1972. *Photo by Tim Bullard.*

"Asphyxia due to rope strangulation and drowning," reads the immediate cause of death. It's also listed as a homicide. There was a "rope around the neck," the paper reads. The time of the injury is listed as 10:00 p.m. at his home. Burial took place at Pleasant Home Cemetery in the Lomax community of Wilkes County, with Reins-Sturdivant of Boone in charge of arrangements.

I never imagined how deep my sympathy would go until the day I opened my e-mail and found that an anonymous woman had sent me several crime scene photos. Two were graphic. I was stunned, and I was talking with Whitman as I opened them, describing them; he was taken aback, too.

Bryce's autopsy was authorized by Dr. C.C. Dean, medical examiner, in Chapel Hill. There were three people present at this autopsy. The type of death was listed as "violent or unnatural." He was fifty-one, white, male, sixty-nine inches, 190 pounds, blue eyes, with gray hair. His blood type was O. There was blood in his nose and mouth, with teeth in relatively good repair, the report showed. There were three parallel depressions in the skin on the back of his right wrist, similar to a depression across the anterior chest. There was also a rope burn on the anterior and left neck about six inches long, as well as a one-inch superficial contusion on the right forehead.

He was wearing underpants, an undershirt, a blue shirt, pants and socks and had a right shoe (untied), a left shoe (tied), a pocketknife, a watch, a ring, a handkerchief, a change purse, clean fingernails, fingerprint ink on fingers, subconjunctival petechiae and middle ear hemorrhage; also found on him was a nylon cord that was fashioned as a noose.

The pathological diagnosis was rope strangulation, rope burn of neck, aspiration of water, pooling of red blood cells in the lung, with fatty change of liver listed as incidental. The toxicology was negative for alcohol, acetone and barbiturates and negative for the urine with organic bases.

The probable cause of death was listed as "asphyxia due to rope strangulation and drowning." This would be a terrible way to go, and one might only recall any Alfred Hitchcock film to realize what harsh punishment this would be—a crueler way to go than gunshot, poison or a fall. Clothes and rope were taken into evidence, according to William Pierce of the SBI.

The "stomach contains relatively large quantity of food material, including well-masticated portions of corn, squash and light colored meat resembling chicken. Relatively small amount of well-digested material in the small intestine. Colon contains a moderate amount of fecal material." In his bladder were about ten milliliters of clear amber urine. In the lung, "[b]lood is present in many areas." In the liver, the "sinusoids are mildly congested with blood." The stomach contents indicated "a bird such as chicken."

The summary and content tell you a lot about this crime:

On Feb. 4, 1972 at approximately 10:30 p.m. Mr. Troy Hall and Mr. Cecil Small found Mr. and Mrs. Bryce Durham and their 18-year-old son Bobby dead beside a bathtub with their heads in the water.

They had responded to a phone call that Mr. and Mrs. Hall received approximately half and hour before. Mrs. Hall is the daughter of the Durhams. The call, presumably from Mrs. Durham, was a woman's voice which in a muffled tone asked for help and said that intruders "have got Bobby and Bryce," the phone then went dead.

The scene showed some disruption of furnishings about the house. A four-wheel drive vehicle belonging to the Durham's was found approximately a mile away with some of their property in it. Some blood was found in the living room. A nylon noose was present around the neck of Mr. Durham.

No other ropes or ties were present on the body or elsewhere in the house. Dr. Clayton Dean of Watauga County was the County Medical Examiner. He referred the bodies for autopsy. These were performed together by Drs. Harry Taylor, Abdullah Fatteh and Page Hudson.

External examination revealed no evidence of a struggle except for presence of a moderate amount of blood in the nose and mouth. There was a very small and superficial bruise on the right forehead. An additional exception was the "rope burn" on the neck, particularly the left side.

Internal examination revealed no deep hemorrhages in the strap muscles of the neck beneath of the rope burn. Lungs were congested and edematous. This gross appearance, as well as the microscopic characteristics, are typical of freshwater drowning, although the change is certainly not a specific one.

There was no other disease process to account for illness or death. In my opinion either the strangulation as evidenced by the rope burn and the noose or the aspiration of water as indicated by the lungs and history would have been adequate to have caused death. Toxicological studies to date have ruled out the presence of a wide variety of drugs and chemicals.

Durham was sixty-nine inches, and a body diagram showed a slight bruise to the forehead, as mentioned, as well as depressions on the chest and lower-right arm. Hudson signed the document on February 7.

This is the original bathtub in which the three Durham family members were dumped headfirst so many years ago with callous disregard for human dignity. The crime scene photos taken by local photographer George Flowers were grim. *Photo by Tim Bullard.*

Three ghosts watch me now.

On Saturday, February 5, 1972, the *Orlando Sentinel* ran with the headline, "3 Bodies Found In Bathtub." It was a United Press International Sentinel report. "The bodies of three members of a locally prominent family were found crammed into an overflowing bathtub in their fashionable home, but police said Friday an autopsy would be needed to determine whether they were beaten to death, strangled or drowned," it noted. The article listed Durham as co-owner of the dealership.

Hall is quoted in the article, saying that he had received a call from Mrs. Durham: "There are three blacks in the house. They have Bryce and Bobby in the back room," he said that she said. His home was listed as being two miles from the Durham home. The actual word used was the n-word, according to police reports. "Travel was slow," he said, "because ice and snow coated the mountain roads." He arrived to find the bodies around 11:30 p.m.

The article quoted Sheriff Ward Carroll as saying that the apparent motive was "a grudge." It also reported there was a bank bag found at the split-level home with receipts from the dealership and that it was untouched. "Wallets belonging to the victims were found near the bodies, however, and apparently had been emptied," it read. "The television set was still on, and a telephone on the lower level of the house was torn from the wall. Police theorize the intruders caught Mrs. Durham talking on the phone and yanked it out."

The article reported that the four-wheel-drive vehicle in the ditch a mile away had dealer's tags. "Carroll said it apparently was used as a getaway vehicle," the UPI report read. "The family came to Boone about two years ago from Mount Airy in Surry County where Durham was the manager of the Mount Airy Loan Co.," the UPI Sentinel article read. "Durham had been to a civic club meeting a few hours before he met his death," the story read.

Virginia Dare Durham was born in North Carolina on October 24, 1927, according to her certificate of death. Her Social Security number was 245-34-0202. She was a bookkeeper at an automobile dealership. Her father was Calvin Church and her mother, Jennie Eller Church. She was sixty-eight inches and had blue eyes and blond hair. The cause of death was listed as ligature strangulation and a homicide. The death certificate noted that the death was from a rope around the neck. Her strangulation was diagnosed by hemorrhage into strap muscles, petechial hemorrhages of the eyelids and congestion of the lungs. Also noted as an accessory finding was

Hashimoto's thyroiditis. Her blood type was O. Her rigor was listed as full. Her gastrointestinal tract contained a "large quantity of partially digested food, corn, squash, white meat," noted the certificate.

The medical examiner's report noted:

> *At autopsy there was a ligature strangulation mark around the anterior portion of the neck. Small hemorrhages were present in the strap muscles beneath the ligature mark. The thyroid cartilage and hyoid bone were intact. A small linear abrasion was noted on the right side of the chin, and there were petechial hemorrhages beneath the eyelids. The lungs were congested by not edematous.*
>
> *There was no edema fluid in the trachea or bronchi. Toxicology studies were negative for blood ethanol or other volatiles. The body diagram showed an abrasion on the chin and small bruises on both knees, plus purple lividity of the face.*

Bobby Joe Durham was born in North Carolina on May 2, 1953, making him eighteen when he died. He was single, never married, a freshman student in college at Appalachian State University in Boone. His Social Security number was 247-78-5794, according to his death certificate. His immediate cause of death was listed as "asphyxiation due to strangulation and possible drowning." A rope around the neck was listed as how the injury occurred.

Bobby Joe was wearing a brown shirt, long-sleeved; a white T-shirt; a pair of khaki trousers with a black belt; a pair of white underpants; a pair of brown socks; and a blue stone ring. He had a "brown envelope with money (not opened)." He also had a wristwatch on his left wrist showing the current time and date. There were ligature marks on his neck and face, with petechial hemorrhages in conjunctivae and skin of the eyelids, undersurface of scalp and larynx. There were also pulmonary congestion and edema, listed as severe. Also there was "presence of froth in the air passages" and congestion of visceral organs, plus hemorrhages in the middle ears. His blood type was O. His probable cause of death was listed as "asphyxiation due to strangulation and possibly drowning." The surface of his heart was "glistening."

"Both lungs were large and ballooned," the death certificate reported. "When removed from the body, the lungs retained their shape. Surfaces were glistening and of mottled purplish color." His stomach had one hundred grams of whitish digesting food material but no water. His bladder contained 25cc of clear urine. The final summary reported that there were

Not many Appalachian State University students know that one of their fellow students was murdered in a heinous killing in 1972, and probably still fewer realize that not many people know that the culprits have never been brought to justice. *Photo by Tim Bullard.*

"obvious rope burns on the neck and on the face…The anterior aspect of the front lower gum was lacerated…Both nostrils were filled with froth… It is entirely possible that the decedent might have been strangled while his head was being held underwater and that drowning might have contributed to the acceleration of death." Bobby Joe was sixty-eight and three-quarters inches long.

On Bobby Joe's death certificate, a narrative reported this: "On the evening of Feb. 3, 1972 somewhere around 10 p.m. the son-in-law of the Durham family received a call in hushed tone saying 'the (N-word plural) have Bobby and Bryce' and the phone went dead."

"The boy Bobby had been placed in the tub first, followed by his father, and his mother last. There were rope burns around all three victims' necks with the rope still remaining around Mr. Durham's neck. Both Mr. Durham and Mrs. Durham had evidence of having been struck in the nose before death," it reported. "There was a large gag mark on the Durham boy's face and mouth…The house itself had been ransacked, unknown items had been taken, but a money bag remained in obvious view in the dining room. The police are investigating the motive and suspects for murder."

Dr. Clayton Dean of Boone, the Watauga County medical examiner who responded, talked about the case. "It's been a long time," he said. Has he ever seen a case like this? "No," he said. "Or since." Was it snowing when he arrived? "Yeah boy," said Dean, a Georgia native. "Snowing and frozen and cold."

He had no idea what he was walking into. All he knew was that there would be three bodies awaiting his arrival from the elements.

"I wasn't on call that night. We were playing poker at another doctor's house. I knew three people were dead." Dean thought it might have been deaths related to a gas stove. "It was below freezing. It was cold and windy. I had on leather-bottom shoes. I couldn't walk up the driveway. I couldn't walk. I hadn't planned on being in the snow. The police were there. Three of them were kneeled over the side of the tub. The water was still running." Three ghosts watch me now.

Did one person commit this crime? "I don't think any one person could do it," said Dean, pointing to the size of Bobby Joe. "He was a football player. He was a big boy. One fellow couldn't have done that. I don't know why. I think there was more than one person involved."

Dean does not believe that the crime will be solved. "These kind of people are bad people. I don't think they are walking around hiding somewhere." Could the murderers do it again? "Oh yeah. I don't have any doubt." Who does he think did it?

"There was a lot of scuttlebutt. For a long time they thought the son-in-law was involved," Dean said.

The Saturday morning paper of the *Winston-Salem Journal* in Winston-Salem printed on February 5, 1972, cost one dime and was twenty pages for this Pulitzer Prize–winning newspaper in its seventy-fifth year. Jesse Poindexter wrote a lead article on page 1. The lead paragraph reported that three men were being sought for the slayings of the family of Mr. and Mrs. Durham, owners of Modern Buick Company. Hall received the frantic call at 10:30 p.m., it read. "The investigation has definitely centered on these three Negro men," Carroll told the paper. The Durhams were Wilkes County natives, Poindexter wrote, from the Lomax community.

Pleasant Home Baptist Church's graveyard in Wilkes County's Roaring River section is the final resting place for the murdered Durhams: Bobby, an Appalachian State University student; Mrs. Durham; and Bryce Durham, the father. *Photo by Tim Bullard.*

"About 10:30 p.m. Troy Hall received a telephone call from Mrs. Durham, who told him that three Negro men had 'Bryce and Bobby' in a back room of the house, beating them," the paper reported. Pictures were torn from the walls, the reporter said. Hall found the home with bedding ripped off and piled on the floor, a pool of blood located in the den. Poindexter let his readers know the time of Hall's call to the Boone Police Department: 10:50 p.m.

Wilkes County residents will talk to you about this crime. "I'm related to them. I never did know much about that. It's just sort of a mystery. We are distant cousins," said Charles Durham. "I really wish they could find out more about what happened." Another relative talked as well. "We are related. I felt bad," said Hayden Durham, sixty-seven. "I felt bad."

Frances Durham, seventy-one, of Greenhorn Road said, "It really tore that family up. My husband and him were first cousins. They were at my house a week or two before they got killed. I knew Virginia and Bryce. His sister and I worked for the Democratic party for years. I just remember them being good people. They would come to our house. I hope they can find out who did that. That was terrible. I went to the funeral. I remember it was so sad." She said that there were a lot of people at the funeral. She could tell that there was a lot of makeup used. She also added that she had heard that the son-in-law was mean.

A man who lives near the church gave directions to the cemetery, and he repeated the remark she made about the son-in-law being "real mean."

E.J. Durham Jr. talked about the father. "I would be a first cousin because our fathers were double first-cousins," he said. "We're all a real close family really. Bill is the only surviving brother of Bryce Durham. Bill lives in Wilmington. I still live in Wilkes County. I'm a retired probation and parole officer here in Wilkes. I worked Wilkes and Alleghany until I retired. I've been retired for twenty years."

Durham, seventy-four, remains active and has a cattle and poultry farm now with his son. "We have a Durham cemetery about two or three miles from here that all of our family is buried at," he said. "It's been a long time ago when this incident happened. I taught school at Wilkesboro Elementary from 1968 to 1967. I remember the fact that it was cold, wintertime."

"Bryce, he served in the navy during World War II," he said. "He and my father were, at least for a short period of time, involved in a business together. Then Bryce, he owned the Buick dealership in Boone. I did not know Bobby that well. I knew his father much better. I don't know what happened to Bobby's sister, who was married to Troy Hall at the time. I heard that she was teaching school in Yadkin County at one time. I think she's been estranged from the family ever since that happened."

"I don't have any opinion as to anyone's guilt or innocence. I just don't know enough about it to form an opinion as to what actually happened," Durham said, continuing. "I do know that they were not cooperative. That puzzled the investigators."

What about Bryce? "Bryce was an intelligent, hardworking person. He really apparently did very well after he came home from World War II. He was a easygoing, mild-mannered person," he said. "He married Virginia Church and lived in the community of Purlear, North Carolina.

"Bryce was a good Christian. He had a good Christian family. His father was Coy Durham. Coy was a retired schoolteacher and a principal," he said. "He came from a very good family. Bryce's mother was the postmistress of the old Lomax Post Office. His sister passed away several years ago. She was a schoolteacher. She was good at singing and playing the piano. I believe she had cancer."

There is a lot of history to this small country church in Wilkes County, where there are tombstones for the three murder victims from Boone. *Photo by Tim Bullard.*

"Her husband is a Mauldin. He passed away just a few months ago. He was retired from the U.S. Air Force," he continued. "They have two children who live out there. One son lives in the old Coy Durham house. It's a nice-looking old house. Bryce was a good businessman, and to my knowledge he did well after he left Wilkes County, but he stayed here for a while."

What about Mrs. Durham? "Virginia grew up in Purlear, North Carolina, up U.S. 421 toward Boone near Millers Creek. You pass right by it on the old road there. She was a very attractive blond, probably five eight or nine," he said. "I don't know much about her personally. I just remember seeing her with Bryce and that she was a very attractive, pleasant lady to be around."

How did the tragedy affect him? "I believe it had a tendency to bring the family together. We did anything we could do to help the situation as far as solving the crime. It's been on everybody's mind since February 1972. Almost on a daily basis," he said. "I know Bryce's father and mother, that was the main thing they wanted out of life before passing away was to get this solved and have the people brought to justice which did not happen in their lifetime."

"I think the number one priority or wish was to get this taken care of, to put it behind them. Coy lived to be ninety-five or ninety-six years old," he said. "He lived a long life, but he still did not live long enough for the crime to be solved. It's affected everybody in that it's still on our minds. Bill Durham, the only surviving brother—I'm sure he feels that way today."

How does he feel personally? "I don't know. I don't want to point a finger at anyone. The only thing I think may be the fact that they were apparently not cooperative in this situation, the Halls. I do remember one thing that [an SBI agent] told me. Apparently, there was something said about some black men, and I'm not a racist person. I voted for Barack Obama and am proud of it," he said. "I'm not a prejudiced person, but there was something said about some black men being in the house and a telephone call that was made to them and said that there are so many black men in the house killing Bryce and Bobby. They used the n-word. [The agent] specifically told me that they vacuumed it and cleaned that whole house and there was not one single hair that came from a black person."

Will it ever be solved? "Not unless somebody makes a deathbed confession," Durham said. "I don't have any high hopes. If you don't solve a crime within a few days or weeks, I guess it is difficult to solve."

How would he feel if it was solved? "I think everybody, not only the family, but everybody in Wilkes and Watauga County would be extremely pleased about it. They deserve a lot of credit for staying with it for so long. Back then DNA was a nonfactor and had never been heard of back then."

He has heard of the Halls and went to school with some of the older Halls. "Troy's family grew up here in Wilkes. To my knowledge, they were all good people. Ray was an older brother that married one of my former students," he said. "I don't have any animosity toward the Hall family in any way. They are all good, hardworking people to my knowledge…somebody did it, you know. It didn't just happen accidentally." Soon three ghosts will leave me if this crime is solved.

Could the killers do it again? "I don't know. I don't know the motive or the circumstances. I do know it was something brutal that happened. I don't know if it was a robbery. Somebody stood to gain something. I don't have a clear motive in my mind. I couldn't imagine somebody doing something like that. It's just beyond my comprehension," he said. "People on the spur of the moment do commit a violent crime. As far as planning and carrying this thing out in a deliberate way that they did, it's just kind of beyond my comprehension."

How would he describe the killers? "I definitely think they were coldblooded. As I understand it, they apparently put a rope or a nylon cord in the mouth of Bobby. If you're going to take somebody and put them underwater and hold them until they are dead, I don't know. I couldn't imagine holding somebody underwater until all the life had gone out of them. That's about as brutal as you can get. You would do them a favor if you shot them between the eyes, I suppose."

If the killers were caught, would they be eligible for the death penalty? "Oh yeah. I'm very much for the death penalty, not only in this case but in other cases. I'm certainly a supporter of the death penalty. Some people

This is the Durham family's headstone in Wilkes County. *Photo by Tim Bullard.*

might call me a liberal. I swing from one way to the other," he said. "When it comes to the death penalty and to law enforcement, I'm just as conservative as anybody. I am not a conservative. I am not a liberal. I will swing one way to the other on different issues, that's sure."

Durham seemed like a trustworthy person to interview. He was in the first graduating class of Wake Forest University in 1957.

Durham hopes that there will be more press coverage of the case. "It needs to be brought back to the forefront so it will be on their mind," he said.

It's a cool Saturday afternoon. Touching the white ceramic surface, it was like a jolt, connecting me with a moment in time. Graveyards can be chilling, even in the daytime. And there they were. In the picturesque community, a bucolic setting where green pastures meet azure sky, Wilkes County seems like part of God's country. Tucked away on a back road in the country, there were three gravestones in front of me, cold to the touch, symbolizing what I have researched and written about for so long. They follow me. They greet me in the morning. In the back seat they follow me down the highway. At night you can almost make out their figures in the darkness, waiting, beckoning for me to do more. In the sunshine, I say a prayer for them and for me as my wife and I continue our trek to the Annual Brushy Mountain Apple Jam and Festival in downtown North Wilkesboro, where the smell of grilled food fills the air.

The words of Mrs. Coffey keep coming back to me. "I hear footsteps running up and down the steps sometimes," she said. "I'm not afraid of them. I don't feel like it's a scary presence. I do feel something. I believe there are spirits that are lost. I do believe in them. When I'm laying down in my bed, I can feel someone laying there beside me, and there is no one there. It's the same exact bathtub still."

THE DEVIL AND TAKING THE EASY WAY OUT

Trembling, the trucker's finger slipped into the loop of the gun as his vehicle was parked on the side of the road near some of the world's oldest rocks near the Tenneseee line. He then pointed the weapon at himself. Time was quickly running out. He was about to become a ghost.

The worst thing you can do in life is to do something that hurts everyone you know. Yes, many of us think about it. One of the most prominent figures in the Bible is a guy who decided to take the easy way out. This fellow had a pretty good reason for doing it, however. We always figured that if anyone ever was accused of killing the son of God, suicide would be a perfect solution for that person.

It is a choice that may seem like an easy answer. As an impulsive decision, sometimes it may be the most dangerous if someone has bumped into a shattering incident that overwhelms with tragedy, a demonic incident of fate that is just too unbearable and unfathomable to endure.

Judas pretty much ruined the future for anyone with that name. Besides Adolf, all of the first names have been taken except for Mr. Iscariot's title. It's just bad advertising to have a name synonymous with the guy who helped lead to the crucifixion of our Lord Jesus Christ. One would assume that the ultimate sacrifice should be paid by the one who killed Jesus. Were Judas and Jesus in cahoots?

Mob justice rules for bad guys like John Wilkes Booth, Judas, both villains. He was one of the twelve, an apostle. He was a stooge, as JFK's killer called himself a patsy. The chief priests set Judas up, the most famous suicide victim. To look at this act of sole betrayal, it may help us to look at the man who made this crime, and that's what it is—the cruel crimson scar. The priests thought there might be a riot.

Of course, enter the Big Guy, Satan. Luke claims that the devil entered Judas the night before the big feast. It would be very easy to blame the devil for the mental illness that Judas must have been suffering. Lucifer always wants to take credit when no one is man enough to grab it. Maybe he did it for the silver; maybe he did it to be famous.

Deadly cause and effect can cause innocent victims to find their just rewards too soon. They don't deserve it because they are everything we want to be—innocent.

Look at Lincoln. He was just sitting there, enjoying what we know was a comedy. Now, no one in his right mind would enjoy a play, much less in times of war. Being shot in the head might not be a bad outcome if you were bored out of your skull.

When we come to mass suicides, however, there comes a moment when the mental illness reaches a point of no return, the infinite horizon of fire and brimstone. Committing suicide with a nuclear weapon is just about impossible. It's going to be a billion-man party, and invitations are in the mail. One easy way to kill yourself is to kill everyone. That way you take yourself out of the equation, and there is no mess.

Simple poisoning is another route that the unsophisticated suicidal hustler takes, deciding to mask the trail and leave it to the detectives to sort things out. Leaving a mind-boggling trail in the woods that a coon-hunting hound dog could sniff out can fool even the best policemen, but today there are so many high-tech ways to learn who didn't do it, narrowing it down to who did.

At least, that's *if* you are trying to taunt people. Let's say you do not care if people find out who killed you, and you let the evidence point to you. Let's also say you want it to point at a friend or loved one, a person you would not mind seeing spend the rest of his miserable life in prison or on death row. The *Farmer's Almanac* should be renamed *The Guide to Killing Oneself*—or *Never Do It on a Sunny Day*. Some people plan their wedding days by the almanac, finding it is easy to pick a day without rain. Then comes the rope. It is the choice that many men and women take. It's the final curtain call. Some guys do it because they suffer from depression. For others, it may be insanity or religious guilt. For far too many, suicide comes from one too many nights staring into the bottom of a bottle of alcohol. Is it a sin? Thou shalt not kill was not just an add-on. Are people who smoke suicidal down deep? Maybe.

Well, I've covered a lot of suicides for newspapers. I went to one at a campground for the *Watauga Democrat* once, and a guy's brains were splattered all over a picnic table. "Brains and eggs?" the county coroner asked me. The other one was a trucker who had seen no way out of his mortal dilemma, so he did the dirty deed inside his truck's cab. The EMS workers needed an extra hand, so Dr. Evan Ashby, the county coroner, accepted my offer to hold the canvas stretcher as it was scooted out of the tall cab.

I was grossly out of shape, so the full weight of the trucker fell on my arms to balance and lift as the body slid out my way on the driver's side. As it became apparent in short order that the pounds the corpse weighed would be almost too much for me to bear, his head began to rock to and fro, his soft gray hair tickling my wrists as I lowered my end in tandem with the other two guys holding the other end. Some unexplainable force assisted me, and the horizontal trucker lowered without falling from his earthly perch. Whenever something tickles my wrists, I think of the cadaver's hair to this day. Friends of mine have taken their lives, and for the love of God, I cannot think of how things got so bad for them. Was it money? Could it have been the bills?

Some people are forever haunted by the mistakes they have made in life and the sinful things they have done to other people. Maybe they stopped going to church, thinking they could never go back. Losing one's faith is an illusion. One can never lose faith if you ever had it at all. Thornton Wilder best put it in *Our Town* with all the haints talking about a village as the idea of who is dead and who are really dead blurs. You will die. That's what you're afraid of. When you stop doing dangerous things is when you can relieve yourself of the burdens of life. If it is a sunny day, go out and make the best of it. Unemployed? Go out and look for a job. You might get lucky. If night has fallen, rent a scary movie. Libraries hold some of the most frightening volumes of ideas imaginable. But when you turn the lights out, protect your wrists from the wisps of hair from the horizontal trucker. Those who commit suicide are going to hell anyway.

GREEN PARK INN

If you have ever spent the night at the historic Green Park Inn in Blowing Rock, North Carolina, then you know how relaxing this plush monument of an accommodation is. It is not haunted—repeat, not haunted. But it sure looks like it is.

The Cherokee and Catawba Native American tribes inhabited this area around Blowing Rock with Scotch-Irish immigrants in the mid-eighteenth century. It is not haunted, but it is very Gothic, with southern architecture found nowhere else.

There were reportedly two Native American lovers, "one from each tribe," who were walking near the rocks when the man got word to return to his village and go to battle, but his lover asked him to stay. He threw himself off the rock and into the valley, so the lady prayed to the Great Spirit to return her lover, legend says. Then there was a gust of wind from the John's River Gorge, which blew the guy up the cliff to the top of what is now the Blowing Rock.

Having opened in 1882 under the Green family management, the inn has hosted figures like Annie Oakley, J.D. Rockefeller, Eleanor Roosevelt, Margaret Mitchell, Herbert Hoover and Calvin Coolidge. Once Arlo Guthrie gave an interview to a local newspaper reporter, who asked him about his father, Woody, and about solar power. Many famous celebrities have spent the night here. It has recently been renovated.

Across U.S. 321 is the Eastern Continental Divide. The inn is on the National Register of Historic Places, included there in 1982 in its 100th

There are no ghosts or haunted stories about Green Park Inn in Blowing Rock, but its Divide Tavern, open to the public, keeps visitors in touch with the past and a bygone era. There is fine dining with the Laurel Room Restaurant at the Green Park Inn. *Photo by Tim Bullard.*

This postcard—a view of Green Park Inn in Blowing Rock—was published by the Brown Book Company of Asheville (1905–15). *Courtesy of the Durwood Barbour Collection of North Carolina Postcards, Wilson Library, University of North Carolina–Chapel Hill.*

Hugh Morton took this photograph of a man and woman posing on the Blowing Rock.
Courtesy of Hugh Morton Collection of Photographs & Films, Wilson Library, North Carolina Collection Photographic Archives, University of North Carolina–Chapel Hill.

year. It is the second-oldest resort hotel in the state. The town's earliest beginnings started before 1752, when Moravian bishop August Gottlieb Spangenberg visited.

Not far away there were once gunshots from a woman known for her aim. She usually hit what she aimed at. Does her ghost still haunt Blowing Rock?

Across town, with 138 rooms, Mayview Manor was built by Walter Alexander, and it opened in 1921. It was closed in 1966. This hotel was built with chestnut wood and fieldstone, and its exterior was made of chestnut bark. The Boots and Saddles Ball was held here for forty years. The hotel was demolished in 1978. There were billboards for the resort in Pigeon Forge, Tennessee, in 1939, and also Cumberland Gap, Tennessee, in the 1930s and in Greenville, Tennessee, in 1938. "Sensation Rose" was an entry in the Annual Charity Horse Show in 1936. Photographs of the interior remind one of the hotel in Stanley Kubrick's *The Shining*.

Annie Oakley worked at Mayview Manor for the Mayview Gun & Rod Club in 1924–25, according to the director of the Blowing Rock Historical Society. There were one hundred charter members, and the membership was

This is a section of the Mayview Manor ballroom in Blowing Rock, printed by the Albertype Company of Brooklyn, New York, hand colored. It is the view of the large, empty dance floor, with chairs along the edge and lanterns hanging from the ceiling (1905–15). A piano is on a small rise in the back of the room. *Courtesy of Durwood Barbour Collection of North Carolina Postcards, Wilson Library, UNC–Chapel Hill.*

This was an aerial view of Mayview Manor in Blowing Rock, postmarked June 20, 1940. Some say that this establishment was haunted. *Courtesy of North Carolina Postcards, North Carolina Collection, University of North Carolina–Chapel Hill.*

This is the exterior view of Mayview Manor in Blowing Rock (1955) with its lawn, flowers, tables, umbrellas and beauty (photo circa the early 1950s). The photographer was Hugh M. Morton, who took the photograph for the North Carolina News Bureau, Department of Conservation and Development. *Courtesy of Hugh Morton Collection of Photographs & Films, Wilson Library, North Carolina Collection Photographic Archives, University of North Carolina–Chapel Hill.*

$500, according to society director Ginny Stevens. Did you know that writer Jan Karon's "Mitford" series was based on Blowing Rock?

According to High Country Parkway, Annie Oakley worked for Mayview Manor, operating the trapshooting range. Does she still haunt the manor and Blowing Rock? Cone Manor, across town from Mayview Manor in Blowing Rock, was in the opening scenes of *The Green Mile*. Off Aho Road, there was a cemetery scene filmed at Laurel Fork Baptist Church. Annie Oakley was born on August 13, 1860, and she died on November 3, 1926. Her birth name was Phoebe Ann Mosey, and she could shoot a gun like nobody's business. She could split a playing card over and over, putting holes in it before it hit the ground, using a .22-caliber rifle—that's at ninety feet. Beat that. She was born in Woodland, Ohio, and she died at sixty-six in Greenville, Ohio. She was married to Frank E. Butler. She was the sixth of six children, and the family was poor after her daddy died. By the time she was fifteen, she had paid off her mom's farm selling hunted game to folks in Greenville.

Frank Butler bet $100 on her once. He was a traveling show marksman and former dog trainer. Butler lost a match to Oakley and then started dating her. They got married on August 23, 1876. Then they joined Buffalo Bill's Wild West Show in 1885, and she became rivals with Lillian Smith. In Pinehurst, North Carolina, she hit one hundred clay targets in a row in 1922. This uneducated woman taught fifteen thousand women how to use a gun. Her father fought in the War of 1812 and passed from pneumonia and overexposure. Chief Sitting Bull called her "Little Sure Shot" since she was five feet tall.

The Blowing Rock Historical Society wants to keep structures like Mayview Manor around so they will not decay and be lost by the ravages of time, according to Director Stevens.

ONE WATAUGA WITCH

The next tale was passed on from a man named Lindsay Ellison, a gray-bearded farmer of small learning, who had stopped to wait out a bad storm at the home of Thomas Smith, according to *The Frank C. Brown Collection of North Carolina Folklore*. There were about five people present. Someone started a conversation about whether witches really existed. Ellison argued that witches were real, and he told a story to support his argument.

"When I lived below the mountain, I recollect there was an old woman named Mary Townsend, who everyone claimed was a witch," he said. That was forty years before. This story involved a strange shooting match. This was about 1914. Her name was "Ole" Katy Townsen.

"I ain't forgot the time we had a shooting match close to her house. There were a dozen of us fellows, all pretty good shooters," he said. "We got there early to the place where we aimed to shoot. It was right close to Old Katy's house. Out she came and began to abuse us for getting so close to her house to shoot."

The fellows laughed and made her laugh. She told them she would take the shot out of their guns so they could not hit anything. They shot for an hour or two, and after every shot they would check, but not a single shot ever hit a spot.

"We decided to go home, feeling pretty bad," he said. "Old Katy sure had taken the shot out of our guns."

Someone in Wake County said that a witch smeared fat on a broom "in preparation for her flight through the chimney...At midnight an old, old woman dried up to a tiny size, would come down the chimney and sit down in front of the fireplace. She would take some grease from her pocket, grease her hands and behind her ears. Then she would say, 'Up and out!,' and disappear up the chimney."

Do witches change into cats with long legs and neck, a bowed-up back and long tail? Sure. They change into rabbits, too, some say. Not far from Boone in Stanly County there was a report of a witch taking the form of a cat: "There was a man whose horse was sick. He noticed that there was always a yellow cat in the feed trough every morning, so he shot the cat, and in the neighborhood there was a woman playing witch with that cat. She lay up for a long time because the cat was dead, but made out like her arm hurt her."

A lot of North Carolinians have felt down in their hearts and souls that if animals got sick, a witch was behind it, casting spells. "Some claimed they had seen witches enter their homes during the night, get astride their brooms and ride the brooms around the rooms, searching for victims," Brown wrote.

So-called witch men would attend a shooting match to spoil the luck, and no prizes would be won when a witch man was around. Witches could also, according to legend, assume the form of a turkey or fowl. Once a witch man became a turkey, climbing to a limb of a high tree. A hunter was coming home, and he did not know it was a witch. "Every time his gun would fire, the witch turkey would stand erect on his perch, shake himself and sit down again," according to Brown. "The hunter shot 29 rounds at the supposed turkey, not knowing it was a witch." There was no hunter's luck that day.

THE GHOST OF MERLE WATSON

The dark night I interviewed Mr. Merle Watson, the son of Deep Gap musician Doc Watson, his huge, bearlike figure was underneath the *Watauga Democrat* van. Back in those days, as a cub reporter, I was always low on gasoline, and I usually ran out of gasoline once a week.

Merle Eddy Watson was out in Todd at the family's music studio helping a young guitarist record some tracks. Well, I was nervous, so I accidentally pressed down with my left foot too hard on the manual brake, and it became stuck. I was there to interview Merle.

I had interviewed Doc before, once in the green room of P.B. Scott's Music Hall in Blowing Rock, a geodesic dome with great acoustics and a smoky top floor.

Tinkering with the metal parts under the van, Merle had grabbed his toolbox and went to work on cutting the brake cable in two, allowing me to get it back before dawn. So whenever I hear tools rattling in Watauga County, I think of Merle that night and about the fun I've always had at MerleFest, a great music festival created in his honor at Wilkes Community College. This festival was founded in 1988. (Check out www.merlefest.org on the web.)

Sam Bush, a famous bluegrass picker from Kentucky, knew Merle well. "Oh yes, I knew Merle quite well. We started knowing each other very well in 1974 through New Grass Revival. We did fifteen gigs opening up for Doc and Merle," he said. "We did a festival in Kansas in mid-September and went to the West Coast. It was back then that Merle had a band called Frosty

Morn. New Grass Revival would play, and then Frosty Morn and then Doc and Merle and then T. Michael Coleman with them played."

Then he played on a record with Doc and Merle, *Memories*. "I became a good pal of Merle's," Bush said. "He would hire me to play on records he was producing. Many a time we would sit together. Merle was a great slide guitar player." A Kentucky native, Bush isn't too shabby on mandolin either. "His favorite slide guitar player was Duane Allman, as was mine," he said. "We would sit and listen to the Allman Brothers together and marvel at the great slide playing of Duane. I always thought Merle was an acoustic version with the same intensity that Duane had. So, years later I played the slide mandolin."

Bush wrote a tune based on Merle's and Duane's playing, so he called it "Watson Allman." When MerleFest began, Bush said it was emotional, and it still is. "Really, that's how the festival got going. Now, of course, it's grown much larger. We still think about Merle all the time." Bush visited the Todd studio the Watsons had. Bush also played at P.B. Scott's Music Hall in Blowing Rock, a bar that attracted ASU basketball coach Bobby Cremins and hippies galore. "We used to play at P.B. Scott's. I remember Merle coming to hear us one time. It was an odd-sounding room I remember," Bush said. "You could literally be playing and hear the sound man talking on the other side of the dome. It sounded like he was standing next to you during the sound check. So the sound really traveled across the top of that dome."

DANIEL BOONE'S SPIRIT

When one thinks of the great pioneer outdoorsman, the image of Fess Parker comes to mind, a guy who dressed in a buckskin cap. If you are ever hunting in Watauga County, look behind you for the man with the long rifle and hat in the foggy mountain woods, Daniel Boone.

Watauga County remembers Daniel Boone with its colorful outdoor drama *Horn in the West*, a production that has been going on for many years. It was written by Dr. Kermit Hunter, who died on April 11, 2001, in Dallas, Texas. Hunter also wrote forty other production scripts, including *Unto These Hills*. *Wilderness Road* was the title of the drama at first. Hunter attended the Juilliard School of Music. The drama opened in 1952, and it has been seen by 1.4 million visitors.

Actor Glenn Causey played Boone to the hilt for forty-one seasons without missing a performance. The Daniel Boone Theater was built in 1952 in three months, designed by John Lippard and four students from the North Carolina State School of Design with 2,500 seats on thirty-five acres.

"For sixty years we've tried to keep Daniel Boone alive," said Julie A. Richardson, director. "We're very happy that we made it to sixty. It's a blessing. There were several years when *Horn in the West* didn't know if we'd be open again." Alumni members have pitched in.

Did you know that Boone didn't really wear a coonskin cap like the song goes? "That's the Hollywood icon, and we've even been phasing it out of our shows," said Richardson. "They market it that way."

Actor Glenn Causey played Daniel Boone (1960) in *Horn in the West*. *Courtesy of Hugh Morton Collection of Photographs & Films, Wilson Library, North Carolina Collection Photographic Archives, University of North Carolina–Chapel Hill.*

Richardson has been the director for fourteen years. She has been a stage manager and technical director. "It's part of the history of America and part of our freedom. I'm interested in the history of this part of the United States. It's been close to my heart because my parents were in the group of people who wanted to build the theater. It's been in my family. I've been connected to it one way or another since I was a kid."

Unto These Hills in Cherokee, North Carolina, was also written by Kermit Hunter. *The Lost Colony* will celebrate its seventy-fifth anniversary too. Andy Griffith was a member of that cast.

It was on September 26, 1820, that Boone died.

Actor Glenn Causey with *Horn in the West* poses with TV series star Fess Parker. Parker portrayed Daniel Boone and Davy Crockett in television series. Causey played Boone for many years in the outdoor drama. *Courtesy of Hugh Morton Collection of Photographs & Films, Wilson Library, North Carolina Collection Photographic Archives, University of North Carolina–Chapel Hill.*

"With the financial times, it's tough," said Richardson. "That's a challenge of doing the show. We try to do local people. It's a very passionate person who wants to work in outdoor drama. The Battle of Kings Mountain was a turning point in the American Revolution. They do a *Haunted Horn in the West* at Halloween." Every night during the summer, residents can hear shots echo through the forest, leaving a scary feeling as you realize what the wilderness must have been like years ago. The Powderhorn Theater and its environs turn into the "Haunted Horn" during Halloween. The story line pits Boone with mountain settlers wanting to escape the tyranny of the British government. Dr. Geoffrey Stuart, a British doctor, travels with his wife to the colony of Carolina with teen son Jack to study smallpox. Stuart also works with the Cherokee Indians and the daughter of a chief. May 1771 is relived with the Regulators who fight British authorities and are defeated at the Battle of Alamance.

The Southern Appalachian Historical Association Inc. (SAHA) supports the drama and the Hickory Ridge Homestead Museum. The association is a nonprofit member group dedicated to preserving the cultural heritage of the southern Appalachian region.

Daniel Boone's legend stretches into Yadkin County and also into Davie County. It was on April 13, 1753, a long time ago, when a local man acquired his first tract of land in Davie County, according to the *Davie County Enterprise Record*'s article by Gordon Tomlinson printed on July 24, 1975. It was 640 acres, a square mile, on Licking Creek (or Grants Creek or Elisha Creek). Squire Boone bought another 640-acre parcel on December 29, 1753, on Bear Creek, two miles west of Mocksville. According to one man who lived near there, the house was wooden. "It was one story, eighteen by twenty-two feet in size, built of twelve- by eighteen-inch faced logs. The roof was on a sixty-degree slope, and there was only one door. The entire house, including the roof shingles, was pegged together. The heavy plank door, hung on wood hinges, had about eighteen handmade nails in it," he said. "The floor was of heavy oak board edged smooth. The chimney was seven feet wide in front of six feet wide behind, with a very deep fireplace and built of soapstone rocks and wood chinked with mud. A smaller log building, twelve by fourteen feet with a hard, smooth dirt floor and built of round post oak logs, stood near the house. Squire Boone's house would have been typical of the better frontier cabins of the mid-1700s." Squire Boone had sold his farm in Pennsylvania, 158 acres, and came to this state May 1, 1750.

Sometimes, to know a great man, you should research the man who raised him. Below a grave marker in Mocksville is the body of this man who lived a long, long time ago. Back in the day of Squire Boone, it cost five shillings for a wagon and a team with four or six horses to cross the Yadkin River on Bryan's ferry, set by the Rowan Court, and it was three pence for a cart with three or more horses; it was two pence for a sheep or hog.

Between Davie and Forsyth Counties, there were three ferries—one west of Bethania, Glen's Ferry and Shallow Ford Ferry—according to the Moravian Records. There was also Riddle's Ferry nears Idols Dam, which Squire Boone's son, frontiersman Daniel Boone, used. Squire Boone and his wife are buried in Mocksville.

This is the graveyard in Mocksville across the Davie County line that contains the remains of Daniel Boone's parents. This postcard from the Durwood Barbour Collection of North Carolina Postcards is postmarked October 18, 1916. *Courtesy of the Wilson Library of the University of North Carolina–Chapel Hill.*

Squire Boone came to America at sixteen from the village of Callumpton, Devonshire, near Exeter in England with his brother, George Boone IV, twenty-two, and sister, Sarah, twenty.

As the winds get colder on chilly Saturday nights, you may turn the gas heat up a tad to keep warm and wonder how settlers stood it in the freezing winters here. Rum and whiskey were six shillings a gallon in 1755, according to the tavern records in the Rowan Court.

People are often only occupiers of bone foundations if you don't research and share their stories. Squire Boone's story is worth researching. Lodging in a good bed was two pence, and a meal was six pence, according to records in the Davie County Library.

Squire Boone attended court without missing sessions much, and he was one of the justices of the first Rowan County Court of Pleas and Quarter Sessions, which met in June 1753 in Salisbury. Boone met with the court four times a year, according to a 1997 copy of *History of Davie County in the Forks of the Yadkin* by James W. Wall, printed by the Reprint Company Publishers of Spartanburg.

Squire and wife Sarah sold their land in 1759 and moved to Maryland, and they came back in the spring of 1762 and lived at Bear Creek on the property of Daniel. Was Squire living there when he died on January 2, 1765? He and his wife are buried at Joppa Cemetery on U.S. 601 outside of Mocksville. Sarah decided to stay with her daughter, Mary, after Squire's death. Daniel died at eighty-six on September 26, 1820, seven years after Rebecca died on March 18, 1813, at seventy-four.

Go to www.boonesociety.org to learn more. It's really addictive research. Maybe as a youngster you loved Daniel Boone, watched the TV show and had your own coonskin cap. There was nothing more manly than Fess Parker in the 1960s with that cap. This is a false representation, as he didn't wear a coonskin cap like the TV song went, his relatives claim.

This is the story that got me. It's noted in the *Davie County Sentinel and Journal* that Squire was hunting squirrels on Little Knob and saw "the tail feathers of a wild turkey bobbing up and down on the other side of a log that lay in good shooting distance," according to *Compass*, the Boone Society newsletter. "He watched it closely until it proved not to be a turkey, but the feathered head of a Catawba Indian. He put a bullet through the Indian's forehead. Instantly he was attacked by two more hidden Catawbas." Talk about being caught between a rock and a hard place. "He wounded one, and the other, realizing he was a poor match for this old frontiersman, fled for his life."

Daniel Boone died of natural causes. "I'm going now. My time has come," he finally said.

GRANDFATHER TERROR

Everyone loves their grandfathers, and when they are gone, you never realized how much you would miss them. Do you remember the hugs? How about the smell of cologne and whiskers? In Watauga County, there is a strange natural phenomenon in an outcropping of very old rock that has gained notoriety.

My Grandfather Bullard was a tall, large man, a farmer in Scotland County. It was at his and his wife's farmhouse where my family would spend warm, cozy Christmas Days with a house full of presents, Bing Crosby records and rice and gravy to beat the band. I loved my grandfathers to no end, and their hugs still hold me today. I can still bring up the smell of both men from memory.

My Grandfather Sanford was in the navy, and he was superintendent of Waverly Mills, where we would go in the summertime to enjoy barbecue on the Fourth of July, one of the hottest days I would ever experience in my life. He had a tattoo on his arm, and I can still smell his metal fluid lighter.

Grandfather Mountain was called Tanawha or "Great Hawk" by the Cherokees years ago, and Daniel Boone was known to hunt here. In its eighty-sixth year in 2010, "The Singing on the Mountain" here was a gospel singing event that attracts thousands. If you have never visited the Scottish Highland Games here, you are really missing out.

There are twelve miles of trails and five thousand acres here that have sixteen ecological communities, according to www.grandfather.com. You will find a spruce fir forest, the saw-whet owl and the northern flying squirrel. The average temperature is 45.9 degrees.

There are more than twelve miles of maintained trails at Grandfather Mountain, with one hundred picnic tables and grills scattered through the park. The original Cherokee name for the mountain was Tanawha, which means "Great Hawk." Daniel Boone hunted here in the 1760s. *Photo by Tim Bullard.*

Grandfather Mountain is the destination for thousands of tourists every year, with ancient views 5,946 feet high. The travel destination is located near Linville on U.S. Highway 221, one mile from the Blue Ridge Parkway at milepost 305. *Photo by Conor Bullard.*

You won't find vampires here, but the Virginia big-eared bat is here as one of seventy-three rare or endangered species. There is an annual photography weekend here that attracts lens men from all over.

"The United Nations Educational, Scientific and Cultural Organization has formally acknowledged Grandfather Mountain's ecological significance by selecting it as a unit in its international network of Biosphere Reserves," the tourist attraction reports from its website.

The state and the Grandfather Mountain Stewardship Foundation work together to keep the area clear from development, and the state takes care of 2,500 acres of Grandfather Mountain State Park. The foundation keeps an eye on 720 acres for scenic travel. As the wind blows through the suspension bridge, 228 feet high over a chasm of 80 feet, there is a nearby Top Shop with elevator access to the bridge. The Mile High Bridge was dedicated in 1952.

The bridge was built by Charles Hartman Jr. of Greensboro and was reassembled on top of the mountain in three weeks. It cost $15,000 and was dedicated on September 2, 1952, by Governor William B. Umstead. It was rebuilt at the cost of $300,000 in 1999 with galvanized steel and cables.

Kids and adults can enjoy the seven environmental habitats, which include cougars, river otters, white-tailed deer, black bears and bald eagles. If you ever drive up that snake-like road, be careful if there is ice.

THE FEAR OF DEATH

Brown ribbon, its shiny surface spinning, a neon crimson bead the size of an insect eye blinking as the sour smell of three-day-old noodles lingers from a slimy sink, rats scuttling, roaches doing the forty and hurdling motels. Answering machines kill me.

You're crazy to go into journalism. Go to a shrink. Go to a pastor. Update your passport photo. Get help. You're going to need it in this global cage of non sequiturs. Swan diving on the insect couch, I check for the spins with luck, so coherence keeps me conscious as the answering machine rewinds to the beginning of my first message.

Walking in on a live message is always so embarrassing. You feel so very awkward for the caller; it's like walking in on someone else's conversation, psychic eavesdropping. I feel guilty for hearing it late. It's like Daddy said after sixty years without an answering machine: "If you call and I'm not here, call back. You'll get me sooner or later." The real trepidation is when you cannot for the life of you recognize who it is leaving an anonymous message. Cloaked in an invisible hideout, the perp feels safe, knowing that you don't know—or at least hoping that you won't discover his address. "Fear is the parent of cruelty," J.A. Froude said. I wasn't frantic yet, but after I called all of my crazy friends, I knew the caller would remain free from my alarm here in Mullins, South Carolina, miles from Boone. "You're dead. You hear me? You're a dead man," he said.

My Boone editor, Sandra Shook, always used to tell me that it's the threats you never get or hear about that one should be frightened of. But she was never one to get threats because she never was a great editor of the *Watauga Democrat* in Boone, North Carolina. It's why I liked her more than any other editor—it could be that I work better for women, or maybe it was her protective sense. It made sense the first day she told me that, as well as the second time she dredged it out for a rerun, so by the third utterance, the arcane logic of such an editor's twisted logic was revolting and totally inconsistent with known fact, the proven blips on the cardiac EKG of journalism. The *Village Voice* covered that threat in its "Press Clips" column by Cynthia Cotts.

Ears buzzing, I still hear Butch's voice in my grandmother's yard, daring me. "Go ahead, I dare you." I love dares. Proving your insanity can be uplifting. Dares are hard to explain, especially the one born in my home state in 1587. The first yard ape born of English parents on Roanoke Island, Virginia Dare disappeared in 1591 along with the members of the Lost Colony.

Butch and I were only five years old, old enough to know how sweet Grandmamma Sanford's magnolia tree blossoms scented the East Laurinburg lawn, drowning out the harsh aroma of musky North Carolina tar down at the railroad track out front. I had a rock in my hand. It was perhaps the biggest wasp nest I'd ever seen. Gulping, it was impossible to mask my fear as I stepped up to the plate, two yards from the humming hive. Don't ever dare me.

"Here goes…nothing," I yelled, winding back with a fastball that Willie McCovey couldn't hit. Unfortunately, my aim was true, and the rock sank into the soft cardboard shell, signaling the rapture to a few hundred imbecile soldiers that took flight like the monkeys from Oz, butts in the air, stingers dripping poison. My grandmother was making her Lipton's, heavy on the lemon juice and strong enough to pucker the cheeks, and the pressure cooker was whistling over the roast while the pastry, what I called chicken 'n' dumplings, boiled in the steam-filled kitchen. There were turnips boiling, too. "Pot liquor" is what Uncle Norman called it.

My shrieks quickly persuaded my relatives to run out on the porch with quicksilver feet, where the sight of a child's swollen face, ears and throat must have struck the Methodist fear of God into their hearts. Bees have always scared me since that day, and it's hard to forget the pain, surge of poison and delusional madness that turned me into a mush puppet at Grandmamma's. Humming drowned out my shrill shrieks and my family's screams as I ran around the yard in circles, my brain and throat swelling. The wasps are still buzzing in my head.

At first, I was extremely paranoid and lost sleep, imagining that someone was outside my window or at the front door or, worse, the back door. The most frightening recurring nightmare I've ever had that I could recall was one that started when I was very young. It was when my parents and I were living at 315 First Street in Laurinburg, a modest wood home with a front porch, backyard and garage. This was in 1958 or so, when the milkman was still delivering those large-lipped thick glass bottles on the front porch full of cold cow juice. The nightmare would begin and end at different points as I grew older, but the effect was still chilling each time, and wrenching.

I'd be asleep or at home alone, or the only one up, when a knock would come at the front door, which was shielded by an off-white curtain. As I approached the door in my pajamas, I could always make out a shadowy figure on the other side. Sometimes the wind would be blowing. Other times rain pelted the front porch as tree-sized lightning bolts cracked, illuminating this mysterious figure. My tiny hand reached out to grasp the doorknob and unlock it to see who was at the door and answer it. The person is knocking all the time, continuously. It's not loud. It's audible from the living room, a rapping at the pane. Then I start getting scared. I'm terrified and frozen as an arresting force captivates my spinal cord like a bedsheet's tickling my back in a tender spot or something. I'm frozen. I can't move, and I'm standing there like a deer in the headlights. The visitor may be a man. It could be an old lady, but I could never tell. It always seems inhuman with half the anatomy of a beast. Then comes the ghoulish part.

"Who's there?" I sound off.

The intruder is not a force of good, but one of dark evil, a messenger of devilish power. I can't move as the visitor unmasks his sex by laughing this haunting laugh, a loud chortle that reminds me that I'm in a dream because it's not waking anybody else up, and I may be the only one hearing it. I woke many times as a child, perspiring and shaking and crawling in bed with my parents as an earache or illness choked my psyche.

The door begins to open very slowly, and the illumination of the streetlight floods into the room from the front porch, and I still can't move because the figure is black and unreadable. The hideous laugh continues as he walks in closer to me. This is about the time that I've wet the bed, and I'm praying to the cub god of Celestial Seasonings' Sleepytime tea to rescue me and save me by allowing me to seize consciousness and awaken by biting my lip. He always came close to me, but he never actually touched me that I can remember, and I'm glad about that. The dream's end usually came about the time and the age when I became a professional wake-up artist, pinching

This is a campus scene from Appalachian State Teachers College in Boone on a postcard published by the Asheville Post Card Company (1930–45). *Courtesy Durwood Barbour Collection of North Carolina Collection Photographic Archives, Wilson Library, UNC–Chapel Hill.*

myself or grunting in REM. The dark avenging demon never got me, and I stopped allowing him to interfere with my rest process at about age ten. But he's still there, and whenever I have a nightmare now and there is always a figure behind a window in another dream, I know it's him.

In October 2007, the *Appalachian* reported about a ghost. The events were reported by students and staff members in two residence halls on the east side of campus. Coffey Residence Hall was seen by a psychic with blood coming from room 311.

"Max" is the name of the ghost in this hall, which had been a faculty residence hall. The other ghost is called "the White Lady." According to the student newspaper, this haunt floats outside the second- and third-floor windows. East Residence Hall is the other haunted hall, with classroom B18 being known for its stories, including "a shy, reserved professor" who allegedly had a mental breakdown in his office, never to return to the campus.

SEVEN DEVILS IN WATAUGA COUNTY

Everyone from your Sunday school teacher to your principal to your parents has, throughout your life, been hammering into you skull the idea that there is a devil.

This devil has gone by many names throughout the ages, and the devil's persona strikes fear into people like nothing else. Any entity that can take over your soul and control you is one that can make you switch sides of the street when coming into contact with it. First of all, the devil can have a shot at destroying God, or at least some would have you believe it. Temptation is the sin that Satan is most aligned with, as when Adam was tempted in the Garden of Eden. "The devil made me do it." That's the first time this saying was ever used, and Adam had a good reason to with Eve. The Bad Man is also aligned with a serpent, which is a symbol of fear in many parts of the world.

Iblis is who some believe God made out of smokeless fire. You may know him as the Prince of Darkness or Lucifer. He is Leviathan. He is the Dark Lord or 666. You may even know him as Old Scratch. He is "the supreme spirit of evil," reference sources note. He makes his way into a lot of idioms in our speech.

It was in the 1960s that the name for the town of Seven Devils in Watauga County was formed from Indian lore that pointed to the source of the wind's harsh beginning on this mountain. There are still Indian arrowheads found here. Settlement came in the late 1700s.

Town records exist showing that

> *several families lived on our mountain during the next 150 years and the land was primarily used for farming. According to local folk, the lower end of the mountain became known as Mast Mountain and it produced good cabbage, potatoes, and tobacco. In fact, the present Town Hall location was a cabbage and potato patch.*
>
> *The upper end of the mountain was known as Valley Creek including a section known as Buckeye Holler. This area was mainly used for raising cattle. High above the meadows were the predominant geographical features of the mountain, Hanging Rock, Four Diamond Ridge, and Hawksbill Rock, which were named in the early 1800s.*

Seven men on horseback braved an old wagon trail and observed these peaks one fortunate day in 1964. The four Reynolds brothers—Buck, Frank,

Dan and Herb—Ray Smith, George Hampton and Gardner Gidley saw this magnificent mountain as something that should be shared by many. The L.A. Reynolds Industrial District of Winston-Salem, North Carolina, formed the resort in 1965, and the founders were met with the challenge of naming the resort. At this time, there was a rumor about an old man on the mountain who had seven sons "as mean as the devil." People were heard commenting that in the winter the mountain was "as cold as the devils" or "as windy as the devil." The founders wanted a catchy, unique name that would bring attention to the mountain. They noticed the repeated appearance of the number seven, including the seven predominant rocky peaks surrounding Valley Creek, as well as the many coincidental references to "devils." "Seven Devils" seemed to suggest a frivolous, mischievous resort where people could "experience the temptation of Seven Devils."

THE GHOST OF ERNIE LEWIS

It was 1982, and Ernie had just died. His ghost would haunt me for the next three days. Ernie worked at the *Watauga Democrat* newspaper, and everyone would be at his funeral over the weekend—except me. Seven tiny ants crawled out of my computer as I remembered Ernie's everlasting quote to me before he referred me to my landlord on Clint Norris Road: "Fly straight, now Tim." It was the sentence he always said to me over and over, and it has served as a guidepost to life for me, a philosophy that has helped me more than he would ever know. I was late on the rent all the time back then. No overnight female guests was the big rule.

Crackling with intercounty and bleed-over radio transmissions from beyond the Blue Ridge, the scanner on the file cabinet chirped, low on batteries because I had forgotten to recharge them the night before. Having plugged the recharging plug into the wrong hole in the unit, it just played without recharging and turned off without juice.

"10-22 that…[indistinguishable]…off U.S. 321." Barney, the friendly constable, a local police beat cop, stuck his head in to say hello, but I ignored him as the office kidded with him. "Officer down…prisoners sighted off… [crackling] meztirbat sinzkinling…shotgun." They had them pinned in. A few days before, at the Watauga County Jail, two or three prisoners had played a trick on a jailer, who was overcome in a daring escape from the cellblock where they were being held. Two men and a woman had been on the run, breaking into mountain retreats, local residences and other lairs to hide from the law.

"Tell Terry to meet me out there!" I said.

"Which way ya heading?" asked the editor.

"I'll be going out 321 toward the Tennessee state line, but I don't know where after that."

"Remember the scanner! How are you going to cash your check?" the editor asked.

Gunning the Comet, it got the first taste of its illustrious career as a journalism buggymobile. On my desk was my notebook and pen, so I turned the radio up full blast and rolled the window down as my incisors nibbled on the wood and chips of black chalky lead splintered on my tongue in the search for a pencil point.

Before I reached the summit of U.S. 321 Business at the city limits, the blue lights twinkled down the long hill that John and I used to coast down on the way back from the bars in Blowing Rock, cutting off the motor and seeing how badly we could undercut the last record for longest coast toward our place in Vilas. It was the fastest my car had ever taken me down this road, which ices up in the winter so badly that traveling from hilltop to valley floor can sometimes take thirty to forty-five minutes in the intestines of a snow and ice storm.

"A deputy has been shot in the face," the female dispatcher said. Would someone die on this assignment? Faces flashed through my mind like a personnel Rolodex. Who was it? Would they live?

Bottoming out was a rush as rhododendrons rushed by in a green stream. At the Vilas store, one has to slow down to forty-five miles per hour to make the turn safely without jeopardy and avoid the incoming NC 194 Valle Crucis traffic. Payday loot was about burning a hole in my pocket. I lived in Vilas, one of the prettiest spots in the state, nestled between meadows and hills with cows sprinkled across the horizon. "E—F." The needle was nudging into the empty letter's space. Sputtering, the car backfired, as was its tradition, but it would not sputter again for fifty hours after it was to stop.

Last stop for gas, cigarettes and beer before the line and Mountain City, Tennessee, and it was a small store, one that did not seem to be the check-cashing type. Gravel smoked as the tires locked, and the Ford's rear slid within a foot of the gas pumps.

"What's your hurry?" the old cashier asked.

"Manhunt! I need to fill it up, but all I have is my paycheck. Can you cash it?"

"No way. That's too much for me to handle. We don't cash checks, payroll or personal. What were all the lawmen flying through here for?"

"It's the escapees from Boone. Say, what if I fill it up and leave my check with you signed? I trust you. I can pick it up on the way back."

"I suppose so. You work for the *Democrat?*"

"Yeah. I'd appreciate it."

"Well, I reckon it won't matter too much no how. You want me to tack those cigarettes onto it too?"

"Yeah, thanks, and some pork skins too." I looked at the beer cooler. "Fly straight," Ernie whispered to me.

Granite chunks tumbled like dice as I floored it back onto the highway and headed to the turnoff onto which the highway patrolmen were diverting the squad cars.

"What happened?" I asked the trooper. Pulling his shades down his nose, he wouldn't have noticed a machine gun in the front seat because his expression was one of fear.

"Down there, about four hundred yards, they shot him. He's going to go to Watauga Memorial." At fifty miles per hour, an EMS van made the intersection's curve without turning over.

"Get out of here!" he shouted at me.

"I'm history. Who was it?"

I slowed down before reaching the barn, where dozens of cop cars were purring. The next two days were the most exciting days, as close to combat as I would ever get. Snarfing free Hardee's coffee and donated doughnuts from the cops' command station for the next two nights was permissible, a forgivable sin. Around the fire at a nearby station that night, orange tubes sliced the trunk of a van as flashlights illuminated a topographical map that several law enforcement officers were studying.

"This is where they were last seen, at this house, where they took an elderly man and woman hostage at gunpoint. It's their description all right. They're probably run down by now, running on adrenaline, and that's why we need to be very cautious. Look what's happened." Blinded for life in one eye, the deputy would survive, but a public discussion over deputy pay would ensue among the county employees, who could not decide whether the wounded cop was at fault for being shot or a hero for giving them an edge in negotiating higher pay.

"Are you with the press?" the state police officer asked me.

"Oh, that's Bullard."

"Don't mind me. I'll stay out of your way. What kind of weapons do they have?"

The officer took off his hat and rubbed his scalp, smearing back a bad hair day from hell. "A .22, and maybe a handgun; we don't know. You stay close by now. Don't stray off. These are dangerous people."

Dangerous people. I'd heard that one before. The most dangerous people are those people you don't see. Sandy always told me that it was preposterous to be paranoid over someone getting you when it was absolutely every time that you would never see what hit you.

Just then, as I grabbed my left pants belt loop, twisting the volume up, the squelch went back and forth. The batteries were dying faster than a fart in a tornado. And there he was. Slowly pulling into the small parking lot was our excellent photographer Terry, complete with his extensive photography gear and Jehovah's Witness wit. It had been the most embarrassing moment of my life, worse than the dreams about being naked in class, when, while in mid-interview at the Green Park Inn in Blowing Rock, Terry had asked my musical subject a question that was as out of line as asking the queen of England for a temporary loan.

I hate anybody with electric windows. A baseball cap was the first image from behind his truck's door as a big smile told me he was as hot for the hunt as I was.

"Got your new lens with you?" I asked.

"Of course." Terry was empirically proud. He was glad I asked.

"Where are they now?"

Lighting up cigarette number 21 out of 268, I stomped out the one I lighted it with.

"Chain-smoking? That'll do it. Ernie would be proud of you."

"Shut up, man. I don't need that this soon into this thing. Harold told me they fired near this barn over there across the road and headed up a dirt road into a field. The field is surrounded by these two big hills."

"What time was that?"

"About 4:45. Have you got 10:30?"

"Ten-four."

Terry loved the police vernacular like we all did. The biggest way to show off as a reporter is to let as many citizens as possible know that you have committed to memory every police code known to modern Scotland Yard usage.

"You gonna park that heap of junk?" he asked.

"It ran hot on me coming out of Boone. I had to stop and cash my check and fill it up with water."

"You need to trade that thing or sell it like I've been telling you."

"Are you going to bust me all night long? I'm glad you finally showed up. How's everybody about Ernie and everything? It sure is creepy out there. Total darkness. You know I hear these woods are haunted. I bet Ernie's out there somewhere. He's probably watching us now."

"Okay, I think. Everybody chipped in to buy him some flowers."

I was always the person asked at the office to pitch in and never had the money. I was a comptroller's worst nightmare. Without fail, the day before payday there would be a knock on the door, faint, like the one no one ever hears when someone is buried alive. "Can I borrow a few dollars from this week's check? My loan payment's coming up, and I've gotten a little behind."

"If you'd just quit buying that Perrier water and cut back on cigarettes, you might have some money," John would tell me. The accountants humor you, thinking that they might get into heaven a little sooner and for a little bit longer stay, until it gets to be a weekly occurrence, more dreaded than a visit from a Witness during a Super Bowl party.

"How much did you pitch in?" Terry asked.

"Well, ah, you know, I'll owe 'em some on Monday or something."

We drove in his vehicle up the small dirt road, weaving in and out, stopping and doing U-turns, until Johnny Law decided to follow up one lead at about 11:30 a.m. after dozens of false starts.

"Shouldn't we be wearing flak jackets, Terry?" I asked.

"Nah; with that gut of yours, you don't have anything to worry about," the short blond shutterbug said, loading a roll of high-speed film.

"You got black-and-white? Hold on to the color. It doesn't matter if you have Tri-X or some cheap stuff, just as long as you're there for the final moment of glory."

"Really think there's going to be a moment of glory?"

At that moment, as cops returned from the woods, flashlights illuminating the trees, there were one, two, three, four, five, six eyeballs less than a click away, snapping mindshots of their own. The office never seemed the same with Ernie around.

Six months later, the story continued.

"Yeah, we were there man. We could see you the whole time."

Wheeler, the leader, was in a very thick cell in the new part of the courthouse behind the courtroom. Awaiting proceedings waged against him, including kidnapping, assault, jail escape and assault with intent to kill a law enforcement officer, Wheeler's curly hair was lighter than his dark eyebrows and hardened, chiseled jaw. He could beat me up. But, alas, I was outside the cell, and he wasn't even mad at me. What do you ask a guy like this?

"What makes you mad?" I asked, as the jingling keys signaled me that the jailers were unlocking the gray hallway door. His reply was the only occasion in which displayed on the front page of the *Watauga Democrat* was a word that you never hear in Sunday school. Your aunt Floosie will never say it in her lifetime. It's a verb, or a noun, according to how you splay it, and whoever is listening to you when you utilize it is ultimately listening as closely as one can after it is unleashed.

"You mess with me, and I'll hurt you," Wheeler said, unflinching, ready for the next question, which would never come. He used another verb. Crickets crossed legs outside, with owls hooting and twigs snapping from critters.

"What type of faith do you turn to when life gets hairy like this, Tim Bullard?"

"Terry, durnit, if I've told you once, I've told you a dozen times, I don't want to hear this."

"Do you believe in God?"

"Man, if you don't can it, I'm going to break that Nikon."

"You shouldn't cuss so much. You can't go anywhere." He was correct. He had me. A captive audience. I'd feel safer with the escaped prisoners on the lam.

"Tell me, Terry, just how many folks get into heaven? What did you say? About 421 or so?"

"Don't make fun of my religion if you don't have one yourself. You're a Baptist, right?"

"I was raised Southern Baptist, yeah, you know that. Turn the radio on or something." I'm Catholic now.

"Crack that window some. If you're going to smoke, you know you need to go outside, don't you?"

"I need to go to the bathroom anyway. You know, their eyes are like candles out there, Terry."

Terry had won a lot of North Carolina Press Association Awards, and his plaques were gathering dust just like hundreds of others across newsrooms, but he had a golden eye. Whatever happened between the milliseconds it took for someone to make an image from the clusters of wildlife on that border mountainside, when the fuzz flushed them out, to the moment the connection between his mind's eye and his iris to the reflex from his fingerprint's depression to the splash of developer and the cleansing washwave of fixer, he and our lensman Bill Sheffield were the best photographers I've ever met.

There had been a commotion off U.S. 321 in our last hour of retrieval, after missing Ernie's funeral and contemplating death and journalistic redemption and honor. The cops were motioning. Crumpling up the aluminum can, I littered and ran, backup notebook stuffed against the top of my fanny. A gathering of about fourteen cops was somber with no sound effects, with the scanners turned off, until the rattling and metallurgic throat-clearing was intermittently finished. It could be a bloodbath the way they were loading ammo. Disarmed or unarmed, the prisoners made their way, hands behind their heads, from the hill, looking like Methuselah, beatniks, bleeding, black and blue, smudged, smelling of smoke and wearing the looks of doomed cattle rustlers.

"You missed it," Terry told me. He had to rub it in.

Before hitting the sack like an asteroid, I went to John's new apartment above the Sheriff's Department and the jail, where we used to always convene at lunch for a buzz, and told him the entire tale in five minutes, his attention span. Sleep was new to me. It was a stranger. I've always remembered the words, "Fly straight." I still hear Ernie say them.

THE LAST HOLIDAY INN

Someone died in that Holiday Inn room. If you could rewind life and peek in on events from the heavens, this would be a good bookmark to spy on. It was the man who started a fire at the Boone Mall. How did he become a ghost?

"I want to speaka with Teem Boolard." The accent was foreign. I picked up the phone.

"This is him."

"Wanta see all your article on Boone Mall." He was mad about a story I did that he felt misrepresented the identity of a client of Charlie Whipple, whom I see is still an attorney in Boone. He must be doing pretty well after that trial that captured the attention of the entire state. I didn't sleep much after that call. Don't you abhor it when you get a hang-up, and it sounds like somebody's on the line? You pull the blinds, lock the door and check the closets.

A sparrow's beak hammered at an acorn in the floodplain basin near the Holiday Inn on U.S. 321. As its head darted from side to side, it felt the tremor shake the twig it was standing on before its wings parted, grabbing desperately for enough air to warrant a quick climb into the morning air of July. Freedom is the best thing to happen to anyone. It was July 1981. It was pitch-black dark in my bedroom off Clint Norris Road. I had cut the scanner off, but when I got into work, the aftermath of the explosion gave me a destination: the brand new Boone Mall. The Italian Village restaurant had blown up.

At 11:00 a.m. Tuesday, November 24, 1981, the jury finally got its chance. It took about four hours of jury discussion for everyone in that Watauga County Superior Court courtroom to reach a verdict. At 4:33 p.m. the verdict was announced to the court. Judge Ronald Howell warned everyone to be cool, but a defense witness lost his inner strength and began to applaud, which won him thirty days. He had told the court that Christina Altice had sent him letters and had said that she had been promised a deal with the police.

Chief Tester was steaming mad in his office as I interviewed him. It was a big difference from the first time we had met, and they ran a check on me, finding out that I was one of eighteen Tim Bullards in the United States. I certainly hope I was the best looking and smartest. That first encounter was one of the funniest moments in my life. I just learned recently that Chief Tester passed on.

"Who is this new reporter?" Clyde had asked then as other officers filed into his office. I volunteered to take part in a search demonstration and practice with the law in which I was given a gun and allowed to hide out as they doused the lights. One cop grabbed me before I shot at him, and I'll never forget the sharp, painful cuts of steel on my wrists.

"He's with the *Watauga Democrat*, Chief."

A navy veteran, the crusty chief turned out to be a friendly fellow, a good source and a cigarette-smoking comedian. As he rose from his squeaky chair, I swallowed hard, feeling the serious stares of the policemen, I jiggled the keys in my pockets and widened my stance as the chief stopped at the first guy next to his desk, seated. At that particular moment, as the guys were laying out the classified section with wax two offices down, the police chief turned his back to the seated cop, stuck his butt out just a little and ripped out the loudest, longest treble note ever pooted on the fart scale. The entire room disintegrated into loud, raucous laughter as both cops waved the air. I had been indoctrinated and was now part of the club. I must have passed the test.

"What do you think of the jury's verdict, Chief?" I asked him. Stripping the red ribbon from the pack's top, he tapped two cigarettes out as his lips snatched one for a blaze.

"I tell you what, Tim. Give me a minute. I don't want to say the wrong thing. I wish you could print what I wanted to say." His wrinkled forehead translated his feelings for me. "We'll have the type of crime in the city that the people will allow. We have to depend on the citizens to support us in court and our everyday work." He was madder than a skinned polecat dropped in the New River. "If the same thing occurred today, I would not do anything different. We'd do exactly the same thing. It's our job to take it to court, and it is the jury's job to find them guilty or not guilty. I feel like this crime was solved."

Long after the ground quaked, shaking windows and skipping heartbeats for blocks, the investigation by the U.S. Bureau of Alcohol, Tobacco and Firearms, the North Carolina State Bureau of Investigation (SBI) and local law enforcement agencies had been completed.

"We have no apology to anyone," Assistant District Attorney Tom Rusher told me. "We were pleased with the presentation of the prosecution." Tom's courtroom demeanor was always somber but tough when he wanted to be. He used books and papers as props like an actor. But when it came to his final summations, it was "Katie bar the door." Tom would morph into a Bible-pounding southern minister, singing the lyrical legal words, igniting something emotional within the breasts of Joe Juror. Some jurors are smart; some are dumb as the day is long. Tom knew how not to offend either side. His voice would tremble.

"I would like to say that it occurred to me that the police department gave as good an investigation as I've ever seen," Rusher said.

It was seven hours after the sparrow took off for Florida that Hakaj was arrested. They cuffed him at his home, which was not too far from the home of Doc Watson out in Deep Gap. The word "hillbilly" officially has its origin close to Deep Gap. Hakaj had married an American girl from the Volunteer State. His bond was set at $100,000 by Judge Alexander Lyerly on July 23, and he had been released on $40,000 bond, but he was arrested when his bond was jacked to $100,000 on September 2.

His lawyer, a man named Whittle, said that the not guilty verdict was due to "the fact" that the testimony by Gjoni Bardh and Mrs. Altice was "totally incredible." Bardh's next acting role would be later as bloody corpse in a Holiday Inn room in Nyack, New York.

"Look at this! Does this look like I like marijuana?" Bardh exclaimed, answering a district attorney question in the courtroom, standing and pulling up his shirt to reveal scar tissue from the burns he sustained from a flash explosion ignited from what he said was a fire started accidentally from the lighter he used to fire up a reefer. Bardh ended up in a New York City hospital. Bob Kennedy and L.D. Hagaman Jr. from the Boone Police went up to New York to investigate. Bardh was from Albania, having come to the land of plenty of wiseguys in October 1969. He looked like a Russian spy, with a thick handlebar mustache—kind of a Gene Shalit look. They shipped him here from Rikers Island, where they had him on charges in New York.

"I was to burn the place," he testified. Federal, state and local officers were posted at the doors coming into and out of the Watauga County Courthouse courtroom when Bardh spilled the beans. Christine Louise Harrison Altice, eighteen, of Spring Grove, Pennsylvania, was charged with being an accessory with Bardh, who had said under sworn testimony that he planned to marry her around Thanksgiving. He always referred to her as his wife at the trial. The night of the blast, Altice took him to Hakaj's restaurant at 10:00 p.m. for business, he said, and the couple played pool for two hours and went to a Waffle House before the meeting.

At 11:00 p.m., Bardh said that he entered the restaurant by himself. The back entrance had been open, he claimed, and he smelled gasoline near a dumpster outside. Waiting for his acquaintance, Hakaj, Bardh said that he discovered a red cigarette lighter in the back hallway that connected to the restaurant through its back door. It was the ultimate joint. Bardh used the lighter to try to light the joint, and suddenly the hall lights went out, and the explosion took place. The Albanian high-tailed it, burned badly, out of the hallway and outside the mall. There he spotted a policeman.

Stripping off his clothes, the burned man ran to meet Altice at an eating establishment nearby, their meeting place. It was on to Richland, Virginia, for two days, according to Bardh. "Christine took me to New York," Bardh told the court. It was at Jacobi Hospital and Central Park Hospital in the Bronx that he received treatment. A wallet police found outside the mall had a $100 bill in it, which Bardh said Hakaj had given to him for travel expenses.

Bardh, thirty-four, of Washington Avenue, Hanover, Pennsylvania, had also told the jury that Hakaj had allegedly promised him $50,000 from $225,000 in insurance funds after they blew the mall into smithereens. Bardh had been a fugitive from New York justice since 1978. He was also facing assault and attempted murder charged in the Big Apple. In 1977, two Albanian brothers had been wounded in the explosion.

"What's up Barney?" Officer Barney of the Boone Police Department had his hands on his hips as I stepped over rocks, rubble and debris. Barney usually gave out parking tickets on Main Street, known as King Street.

"What in the heck happened?" The blast had severely damaged nearby stores and destroyed the Italian Village pizza parlor. Stores were temporarily closed for a while, including Kinney Shoes, the Chocolate Factory, the China Clipper, the Lettuce Leaf and Take Ten arcade.

Cops were saying that they had found an "indefinable flammable liquid." Roma oil cans had traces of gasoline. Hakaj was twenty-five, and he was the owner and manager of Italian Village. Charges included malicious damage of occupied property by use of explosive or incendiary device. The architect had been J.T. Pegram Architects of Statesville, and I interviewed Mr. Pegram here in Myrtle Beach not too long ago, revisiting the scene.

They had checked out T-beams, walls and steelwork to find out if there was any crippling structural damage. But right slap dab in the middle of the mess came John Downey, a reporter for the *Winston-Salem Journal*. John wrote a blistering investigative piece linking Bardh to the mob. Pennsylvania lost a lot with the restructuring, which eliminated the Pennsylvania Crime Commission. That was John's source for linking Bardh to the Gambino and Columbo crime families. It was one of the best stories I've ever seen written.

There had been dough stuck to the sprinklers in the restaurant. Hakaj had reportedly received an eviction notice from the mall's owner, William Barnett—owner of Boone Mall Ltd. through Barnett Real Properties— shortly before the blast. Hakaj had skimped on the rent since July 21, and a supply company in Bristol, Tennessee, was claiming payment for $15,809.04 in furnishings. Repossession was around the corner. A real estate agent visited Hakaj's home on August 2 and discovered that the front door was unlocked and standing open, with a notice from Blue Ridge Electric Membership Corp reporting a disconnection. The realtor said that he found a .38-caliber handgun inside, wrapped in white plastic, as well as restaurant food cans and an exhaust hood.

"Freedom is the best thing to happen to anyone," Hakaj told me outside the courtroom with his wife, Joyce. Sure is. Bardh is free as a ghost now. Never check into that Holiday Inn room.

DEAD INTERVIEWS

I've interviewed a lot of people who have since died; it's an eerie feeling. One person I never thought I would meet again. It was on the Appalachian Trail in 1974. High atop Howard's Knob, the autumn wind swept through our hair as I outlined my future to a friend, Britt. It was our freshman year. My mother had gone to Appalachian, and I was about to break a family record of graduation by dropping out. We attended concerts at a geodesic dome called P.B. Scott's Music Hall in Blowing Rock about eight miles away. Winters were tests of mortal skill. I interviewed Jesse Helms at the swimming pool at the Boone Holiday Inn. He's dead. I interviewed Merle Watson in Boone, and he's dead.

"You know, one of these days I'm going to interview Charlie Daniels," I said to Britt.

"You're full of hot air. You're just a writer for a small college paper."

"Fire on the Mountain" is blaring from the car stereo as my friend Britt and I are sitting on Howard's Knob in Boone, and the carpet of colors in the trees below us down the mountain is wondrous, brown, orange, red and yellow and soft-enough looking to cushion your drop if you decide to jump. The Department of Energy threw up a windmill up here, but later it was torn down. They were doing a study or something to see if they could turn all of that wind into electricity. Britt could do a great Billy Graham impression.

"They could power up Boone for a week on this wind."

"What do you want to be when you grow up?"

"I don't know. I wanna make a lot of money."

"I don't care. Whatever I end up doing, I just want to have a good time."

"What's a good time? Being a millionaire?"

"Oh yes. Yes. Naw, I'd like to travel. What's a good time? What's not?" Ant-like dots slowly moved an eighth of an inch across the tiny university football stadium from which an echo of fans yelled from across town.

"I'm going to meet Charlie Daniels one day."

"You're full of it, too. Have you got any food tickets left for this week?"

"Nah. I sold all mine for that Bad Company show in Greensboro."

I finally did do it, though. Following is a transcript of my May 1998 interview with Charlie Daniels.

> *TIM: Could you tell me about the Dew Drop Inn?*
>
> *CHARLIE DANIELS: Well, I know there are several places by the name of Dew Drop Inn, but the one I wrote about was totally fictitious.*
>
> *T: What's new in your career and your work right now? What's coming up?*
>
> *CD: We're still doing what we've been doing. We're cutting records and doing shows. We did an Australian tour back in January. We're touring extensively this year in the U.S. Our latest album, I've got two albums out actually, one is a family album called By the Light of the Moon, and one is a blues album called Blues Hat.*
>
> *T: Oh, that's a good one. I've heard it.*
>
> *CD: Well, thank you. We're fixing to go in starting next week and record a lot of the old fiddle songs over again. You know, a lot of those were recorded twenty years ago, and the techniques are better, so we're going to go in and record some of those. Just the same-ol' same-ol', cutting records and playing shows.*
>
> *T: Tell me, why did you change the lyrics to "Long-Haired Country Boy"?*
>
> *CD: Ah, at the time I wrote that it was kind of a tongue-in-cheek sort of a thing, and you know, it got to the point that drugs and alcohol have gotten to be such a horrendous problem with the young folks nowadays that I don't want to do anything that would encourage it, so I just figured I'd change the lyrics to it. I figured it was the Christian thing to do.*
>
> *T: How did you feel when your gospel albums did so well?*
>
> *CD: I loved it. I really put a lot into both of those gospel albums. It's gratifying that people like it. Of course, they're special. Those albums go a lot deeper with me than just being successful. The music is very special to me.*
>
> *T: Where's the Wooley Swamp at?*

CD: Wooley Swamp is down in the center of North Carolina. You know where Elizabethtown is at, by any chance?

T: Yep.

CD: It's right in that area there.

T: Did you ever see the Maco Light? [The light at Maco Station is a ghost light near Wilmington, North Carolina, the birthplace of Charlie Daniels. Allegedly, a railroad brakeman, Joe Baldwin, lost his head in a track collision, and his head was never found. A light has been seen through the years going up and down the track, and people say it is Joe Baldwin's phantom looking for his head with a lantern. The *Wilmington Morning Star* has a morgue file on it as thick as your leg, noting how military specialists have studied it, and there is no answer for it besides swamp gas.]

CD: Oh yeah. I've seen the Maco Light.

T: What was that like when you saw it?

CD: Well, it looked just like a lantern down a railroad track when I saw it. I think they've torn that track up now.

T: Yeah, they did.

CD: I used to, years and years ago, I've been over there a couple of times and seen it.

T: What do you think of it? Is it pretty weird?

CD: Yeah, it's weird, but I'm sure there's an explanation for it. I have no idea what it is. But there is an explanation for everything, you know. It was not scary to me or anything. Of course, a bunch of us went over to see it, you know, and rode up there and looked. It's pretty wild. Have you seen it?

T: No, but my uncle saw it. I'm from Laurinburg.

CD: Yeah. Uh-huh.

T: What was it like working with Dylan on "Nashville Skyline."

CD: Oh, it was great. It was a lot of fun. We did that album in a very short while. It didn't take very long at all to get it done. Everybody was having so much fun on it, we just knocked it right out.

T: Did you ever meet Elvis Presley?

CD: No, I never met Elvis.

T: Of course, you did "It Hurts Me" on the flip side of "Kissin' Cousins."

CD: Uh-huh. Yeah.

T: Do you still get royalties on it?

CD: Yeah, I think every once and a while they send me a check.

T: In South Carolina, the Confederate flag is flying on the statehouse, and everybody is raising Cain about it, and it's a big issue in the legislature. They're talking about putting it down or bringing it down. I asked Gary Rossington when they visited House of Blues here about the flag, and he said it was mostly an issue of pride back through the years with them. What do you think about the Confederate flag these days?

CD: *I think it symbolizes an area of the country to me. It doesn't symbolize anything else. It has to do with a part of the country that I came from. This flag designates what it is. It doesn't have anything to do with slavery or racial prejudice or anything in my book. Unfortunately, there are some people who do have that attitude. They use that flag. There are people that literally hate other people because of their race and will have that flag as part of their regalia. And I think that's what gave it the bad name. But myself personally, I think it's a beautiful flag. I take pride from being from the southeastern part of the United States. You know, I'm up there about seventy miles from where you are—in Wilmington. Actually, if they take that flag down, that's not going to do away with the things people are associating with it. That's not going to have a doggone thing to do with it. It's just going to make it worse. You know, it doesn't seem to bother anybody else that other people use symbols of their prejudice. There are other flags. There are other symbols of prejudice that other people use that nobody seems to bother with but that particular one that they're picking on really well. It's a piece of cloth that designates a part of the country is the way I look at it. I think we ought to forget all the other stuff and just let it be that.*

T: *My wife kids me because when I bought Freebird: The Movie, I started crying. You were at the Palace in Myrtle Beach last year when it debuted on VH-1. What did you think about it the first time you saw it?*

CD: *The movie? I saw it at the Fox Theater in Atlanta when they previewed it. I saw it in the big theater with the big speakers. It was like sitting in a concert crowd. It was pretty doggone incredible. I don't know how to tell you. It was pretty incredible.*

T: *What did you think about Ronnie Van Zant?*

CD: *I loved Ronnie. Ronnie was a good friend of mine. I was stunned. I was shell-shocked when he was killed.*

CONE MANOR

You wouldn't think a ghost would hang around an outdoor theater. Darrell King portrays Reverend Sims in *Horn in the West* with great fortitude and commitment. This Lincolnton, North Carolina resident has developed quite a following for his ghost stories. He loves this outdoor drama about Daniel Boone. Here is a good Darrell story:

I'm sure you already have a number of anecdotes concerning Flat Top Manor and the supposed sightings of Bertha Cone's spirit, but here are a few that don't crop up in every other "mountain ghosts" book. This part of the story was told to me by Hollie Sherrill, a former production stage manager at Horn in the West outdoor drama in Boone. Back in the '70s, when she was working on the technical crew, Hollie was among a small group of Horn in the West cast members who went out one evening to see the manor.

While they were there, they became aware of an older woman looking down at them from a second-floor window, in apparent disapproval. The group members became a bit unnerved and left. When two of the group went back several days later to apologize for disturbing the caretaker, they were told that there was no caretaker and that no one had been in the manor that night. Intriguingly, although Hollie's group apparently never thought to ask, or at least, Hollie didn't say anything about it when she told me the story, when Hollie pointed out the window where they had seen the old woman, it was one of the windows to Bertha Cone's bedroom.

Cone Manor in Blowing Rock turns into a Halloween extravaganza before October 31. *Photo by Tim Bullard.*

That's not the only story Darrell tells. Here are some other good ones:

In the mid-'90s, my friend, Patrick Kirby, was working in the Craft Center on the first floor of Flat Top Manor. One morning, Patrick was in the Craft Center, getting it prepared to open for the day. He was standing at the main sales counter, near a peg-rack of the ubiquitous wooden "mountain toys" sold in nearly every type of shop in the High Country, when an entire peg of "whimmy-diddles" lifted and stood straight out in the air as he watched. Patrick was so unnerved by the sight that he left the house and stood outside until someone else arrived to help him open the shop.

In 1996, I also took a group from Horn in the West to see the manor. We went out late one evening in midsummer to sit on the porch and tell ghost stories. We had been there for quite some time and had told a number of ghost stories, and consequently several of our group began feeling, shall we say, a bit uneasy with the house, particularly one young lady, who claimed to be extraordinarily sensitive to paranormal activity. We decided to leave, and several of us walked her back to the cars, as she was in a highly emotional state. Two of the group, however, a young man and woman who were romantically involved, hung back at the house. We reached the cars, and had succeeded in calming the girl down, when we heard a scream from the direction of the house. A few seconds later, the couple emerged from the stairs into the parking lot, wide-eyed and near panic. They reported having heard a woman's laughter from a second-floor window. I took the female half of the couple back down to the house. The young man refused to go. So much for gender stereotypes. She pointed at the window where they had heard the laughter. It was a window to Bertha Cone's bedroom and, ironically, the same window Hollie Sherrill pointed out to me a few years later, when she told me her story. She began to get agitated as we stood there, and we lost no time in getting back to the cars and from there back to Boone.

In 2006, I took another group from Horn in the West out to the manor. It was on this occasion that I had my own odd experience there. We were standing on the opposite side of the house from Bertha's room this time. If you look at the house from the front, it was the left end of the house, near the entrance to the Figure-Eight trail into the woods beside the manor. As we watched the windows on that side of the house, the curtains were pulled back by a hand, or rather by the lack thereof. I say that because we could see where the curtain was being gripped and see something like a vague outline of a hand, but the hand itself simply wasn't there. The best way I can describe it is that we could see the void where the hand should have been. At the same time, we all got the distinct feeling that we were being watched. Most of our intrepid little band of ghost hunters became spooked at this point, and once again, our group was soon sitting comfortably back in our own apartments.

Incidentally, I take a group from Horn in the West out to Flat Top Manor for ghost stories at least once a summer and have been doing so for about twenty years. The two times I've detailed are the only times when I've experienced anything out of the ordinary.

HOWARD'S KNOB AND
THE GHOST LIGHT

There have also been reports of some type of apparition seen on Howard's Knob, near the observation platform, according to Darrell King. It has been described only as a dark figure of some sort and seems to project an aura of menace:

> One group, ASU students who had ventured into the park after closing time, something they shouldn't have done, as it happens to be illegal, described it as being a dark, cloaked or robed figure with red, glowing eyes, according to a few of the group; the other, a group of friends which had driven to Boone for the same purpose, some from Wilkesboro and others from the Charlotte area, and were also in the park illegally, described only a vaguely discernable human-like figure that watched them from the trees and seemed to be moving towards them, but moving only when they weren't looking directly at it. In both cases, the trespassers swiftly vacated the premises. I can't find any background story to this one, and have only found two small groups who reported actually seeing anything up there, but I've talked to a number of people who have experienced uneasy feelings near the observation platform, including one girl who described herself as psychically sensitive who came up with a group of friends for a picnic during normal operating hours, and was so unnerved by whatever she sensed that she refused to leave the car. She became so afraid of the presence she sensed that the picnic had to be continued at a picnic-ground on the Blue Ridge Parkway.

Horn in the West, the outdoor drama about Daniel Boone, is haunted, according to some who have worked there. It was written by Dr. Kermit Hunter. The cast numbers about fifty, and each night there are local residents who take part. *Photo by Tim Bullard.*

Not far away at the *Horn in the West* venue there are more weird happenings, he claimed:

> *It's almost a tradition among theater-folk that a theater, pretty much any theater, is supposed to be haunted. Most theaters keep a single bulb burning onstage when the theater is closed. It's considered a part of safety regulation, to keep an unwary person from falling off the front of the stage, but it arose out of a custom to placate the spirits of a theater. This single luminary is known as the "ghost light."*

Sometimes the ghost light has a wire cage. Some say that the ghost light is there to make ghosts feel at home or to make them go away. Some think that it is to keep ghosts of former performances away. Darrell continued:

> *The stage at the Horn in the West outdoor drama in Boone is no different, though our ghost light is a streetlight-type lamp at the top of the amphitheater, rather than a light sitting directly on the stage. Yes, Horn*

in the West has the requisite number of odd noises, moving doors and objects, voices in the dark and other such trappings of a structure that has occupied the same site for a good many years. 2011 has had its sixtieth consecutive performance season. The difference here is that many of us actually know our ghosts. I have spent every summer for the better part of my life on the Horn stage. In 1993, after having already spent several summers in the show, I took over the role of Reverend Isaiah Sims, a comedic but stouthearted circuit-riding Baptist minister who befriends Dr. Geoffrey Stuart, the protagonist of the show.

Because of the complexity of our costumes, Daniel Boone and I are usually the last ones out of the dressing room at night. One evening in 1995, as we were getting ready to leave, one of our costume assistants came running into the dressing room. Her eyes were wide, and tears were streaming down her face. She was shaking like a leaf as she told us of having seen a man sitting on a bench backstage. As she got closer, he was no longer there. He hadn't gotten up and walked off. He had simply stopped being there. She described a large, heavy, older man with a long white beard, wearing a black coat, who simply sat there looking off into the woods until the moment he disappeared. Glenn Causey, who played Daniel Boone at the time, as he had for forty-odd years, just smiled and put a comforting hand on her shoulder.

"Don't be afraid," he said, "It's just Charlie."

A tall, heavy man. Black coat. Long white beard. Go to Horn in the West in 2011. Give that description to our artistic director, Julie Richardson, or to our music director and sound designer, David Courreges, or to Jenny Cole, who plays the Widow Howard, or to me. I'm the man in the big black coat these days. You'll get the same reaction.

Charles Elledge was an absolutely huge man, with a voice to match. He was the first Reverend Sims. The playwright, Dr. Kermit Hunter, fashioned the role just for him. I knew Charlie when I was young, but not really as Reverend Sims. You see, Charlie was Santa Claus. Every year, at Gaston Mall in Gastonia, North Carolina, Charles Elledge would trade the big black coat for a big red one. He played the role to the hilt and once even won a contest ran by the National Enquirer to find the best Santa in America, and the role didn't end at the mall door in December. After the show at Horn, when we invite the audience up on stage, Charlie would often single out a child, kneeling and asking, in that gentle but booming southern baritone, "Did you like what I brung ye for Christmas?"

Actor Charles Elledge (1960) is known to have stalked the stage at Horn in the West, according to one cast player. The stalking was done after his death. He played Reverend Sims for many years until 1983. *Courtesy of Hugh Morton Collection of Photographs & Films, Wilson Library, North Carolina Collection Photographic Archives, University of North Carolina–Chapel Hill.*

Sadly, dear old Glenn Causey joined his old friend Charlie on the other side a few years later. We haven't yet had anyone see a tall figure in buckskins, with a wise, craggy face and a coonskin cap, but I'm expecting it any time now. I don't really know why Charlie seems to be present in the theater after all these years, except perhaps that Horn in the West is the place where he was happiest. I know that's true for me. In any case, if you should come to see our show, and should happen to see a big man in a big black coat with a long white beard standing back in the shadows, don't be afraid, it's just Charlie.

Hickory Ridge Museum

Darrell King continued about Horn in the West and its hauntings, and he explained why cabins can be haunted.

At the top of the hill above the Horn in the West amphitheater, there is a collection of old cabins that has been gathered in that spot to keep them from being destroyed on their original sites. This is the Hickory Ridge Living History Museum.

The oldest building on the property is the James Tatum Cabin. Records indicate that it was probably built some time before 1785, in the area that is now Todd, North Carolina. It was in that year that James Tatum purchased the land on which the cabin stood from Mr. Thomas Farmer. It stayed in the Tatum family through successive generations until it was donated to the Southern Appalachian Historical Association around 1956 and was moved to its current site. Because it is the oldest cabin at the museum, it is associated with the most stories.

One popular story from a few years back is that, during a hard winter during the American Revolution, several of the Tatum children died, and because the ground was frozen so hard, they had to be kept in the upper loft for several months until the ground softened enough for burial. It is, then, these poor children who have been heard moving and bumping around in the upper loft of the Tatum Cabin. Rubbish.

In the first place, The Tatums didn't buy the place until 1785, five full years after the Revolution ended; there was no "hard winter during the

Phantoms allegedly prowl the Tatum Cabin at Horn in the West. The cabin was built about 1785 and was home to five Tatum generations. *Courtesy of Hugh Morton Collection of Photographs & Films, Wilson Library, North Carolina Collection Photographic Archives, University of North Carolina–Chapel Hill.*

American Revolution" for the Tatum family in that cabin. What's more, the Tatums were an uncommon family for the time in that all ten of James and Amy Tatum's children lived to adulthood. Moreover, storing bodies in the loft is a compelling story, except for the fact that the Tatum children actually slept up there. The parents wouldn't have put dead bodies in their children's bedroom, and even if they had, the loft is directly over the fireplace. The rising heat would have thawed the bodies and hastened decomposition. The place would have smelled to high heaven.

The truth is, we have absolutely no idea what the noises in the Tatum Cabin are, although they have been heard by a number of people, myself included, who have spent the night in the old cabin, a practice fairly common among the museum staff. All we know is that they sound far too heavy to be made by an animal such as a squirrel, raccoon or opossum. They seem to move from the far side of the loft toward the ladder access to the main living area and then stop, only to start again a few minutes later, and they have occasionally been upsetting enough to cause overnighters to lose sleep.

Another of the old cabins is the Tom Coffey House. It was built by a professional house builder named Jules Triplett, who lived in the Aho area of Watauga County, for the wedding of Tom and Ellen Coffey. A feature of this two-story cabin is the series of Roman numerals carved into the ends of each of the structure's logs. The cabin was constructed first on Mr. Triplett's land, then disassembled, transported to Mr. Coffey's property and reassembled there. The Roman numerals were a guide for putting it back together—a prime example of early American prefabricated housing.

The poltergeist-like activity in the Coffey cabin takes the form of a "phantom smell," that of burning pipe-tobacco. There is no actual smoke reported, just the sweet aroma of the tobacco lingering both on the first floor of the cabin's interior and on the back porch. Many people over the years, including as recently as July 2010, have reported experiencing the scent, as strong as if someone were standing beside them with a pipe, when no one around the museum was smoking. Like the noises in the Tatum Cabin, there has, as yet, been no explanation advanced for the spectral aroma in Tom Coffey's former abode.

At the top of the hill at Hickory Ridge stands a small cabin, which, due to the particulars of its construction, may well have started its life as either a church or a schoolhouse. For many years, it was called the Weaving House, and the museum's loom was set up within it. Recently, however, the loom was moved into the Coffey cabin, and the building was reset as an example of a found-space hunting cabin. In this house, unexplained voices have occasionally been heard.

In 2004, a museum patron who had stayed behind to look at the loom reported hearing a male voice ask, "Why are you still here?" When he turned around, there was no one else in the cabin. In 2007, one of the volunteer interpreters came screaming down the hill toward a group of other museum staffers. When asked what was wrong, she said she had been opening the Weaving House for the day. She was standing near the fireplace, attempting to light a candle lantern, when she heard a male voice just over her shoulder whisper, "Hello, there." When she turned around, there was no one there. Afterward, the girl refused to ever work alone in the Weaving House again.

Phantom sounds, unexplainable smells, disembodied voices—all classic examples of poltergeist phenomena. If you should visit Hickory Ridge Living History Museum, keep your eyes and ears and nose open. You may get more than a look into the past. It might even come out to say hello.

THE HORSE APPARITION

According to an article on May 4, 1978, in the *Watauga Democrat*, there is a ghost of a captain who still rides a ridge at Riddle Knob. He was hanged in 1781 at Tory Tree in Wilkes County.

The ridge can be reached from a road off SR 194 nine miles north of Boone. There are broken rocks along the ridge, and the entrance is tight, creating need for a flashlight above Elk Mountain and the Snake River and Rich Mountain to the west. You can see the south fork of the New River from this perch, according to the article.

Riddle's Knob is supposedly haunted by the ghost of Captain William Riddle, a Tory. The Wolf Den was his home at Riddle's Knob. Riddle's ghost is said to be seen on board his steed on misty midnight evenings. Riddle was taken in a night raid on the Yadkin River at King's Creek. There was a court-martial, and he was hanged after breakfast at the Tory Tree with two confederates.

If you get up in these parts, you should make sure to visit Yadkin County and its many wineries. Surry County has fourteen wineries and the Andy Griffith Museum. In its first twelve months, about fifty-five thousand people visited the museum. It's called the Mayberry Experience in Mount Airy, where the Blue Ridge Parkway winds around Pilot Mountain. Wine has become such a large part of the economy and tourism that viticulture is taught at local universities.

Winston-Salem is a short day trip to the new Paul J. Ciener Botanical Garden. There is also Old Salem Museums & Gardens. Old Salem was founded in 1766. Reynolda House is a treasure with its museum. The Moravians painted the area with their culture years ago, and even George Washington visited. If you have never tasted Moravian chicken pie, you're in for a treat, especially if you chase it with Moravian cookies. At Tanglewood Park, there is an annual North Carolina Wine Festival, and every year there is the RiverRun International Film Festival. Another day trip is to the Hickory Furniture Mart down the mountain past Lenoir.

CIVIL WAR PHANTOMS

B lue smoke and fiery orange flint explodes from the end of your barrel as the horizon reveals the boots of your enemy flying into the air as he dies before he hits the ground. You are buried deeper than he is, but you are in the same graveyard, within whispering distance, after your bitter confrontation during the Civil War. Watauga County has its share of Civil War ghosts, and Stoneman's Raid was a source of death for its native sons March 28–April 3, 1865. Near Deep Gap in Watauga County there is a Stoneman's Raid historical sign posted off U.S. Highway 421 near the parkway bridge.

According to Margo Metzger of the VisitNC tourism organization, "In an end-of-the-war raid of western North Carolina and southwestern Virginia, General George Stoneman and his cavalry laid ruin to ironworks, warehouses, factories and rail bridges and depots."

According to the North Carolina Department of Cultural Resources Archives and History, Historic Sites, Museum of History and the U.S. National Park Service, "Pushing Sherman's total war approach to the extreme, they burned not only Salisbury Prison (its inmates had been transferred), but stores, homes, schools and public buildings. The raiding continued after Gen. Robert E. Lee's surrender at Appomattox Court House on April 9, 1865. On April 26, as Gen. William T. Sherman accepted Gen. Joseph E. Johnston's surrender in Durham, Stoneman's men were sacking Asheville."

The significance is noted as Stoneman and his raiders "deepened the pain of North Carolina's reconciliation." Suzanne Brown with the North Carolina Department of Commerce, a division of tourism, film and sports development, was at the Annual North Carolina Tourism Media Showcase held at the Lodge at the Ballantyne Hotel in Charlotte on March 29, 2011, with twenty-seven tourism groups represented.

Freelancing an article on a tourism conference can be intimidating until the author realizes that the topic that really sells newspapers and magazines is the Civil War. North Carolina has always pushed the Battle Between the States and its 150th anniversary.

ABOUT THE AUTHOR

Tim Bullard was born in 1955 in Laurinburg, North Carolina. His magazine work includes articles and photographs in *Planning* magazine, *Army* magazine, *Sandlapper* and *Our State North Carolina*, as well as on the John Blue Cotton Festival and others. Bullard's website can be found at www.timbullard.com. He has worked as a reporter and columnist for the *North Myrtle Beach Times* and also for the *Hickory Daily Record*, the *Myrtle Beach Herald* and the *Watauga Democrat*. He has won writing awards from the South Carolina Press Association and the North Carolina Press Association. The South Carolina Senate and the South Carolina House of Representatives both presented him with a plaque of appreciation and recognition for investigative reporting. The *Village Voice* also featured him in its "Press Clips" just before 9/11/2001. An Eagle Scout, he is married to Diane Carr Bullard, and their son is Conor Bullard. He enjoys technology and has written about hardware, software and tech issues for many years.

Visit us at
www.historypress.net